The Depravities of War

SANDOW BIRK

The Depravities of War

HUIPRESS • MAKAWAO, MAUI, HAWAIʻI
GRAND CENTRAL PRESS • SANTA ANA, CALIFORNIA

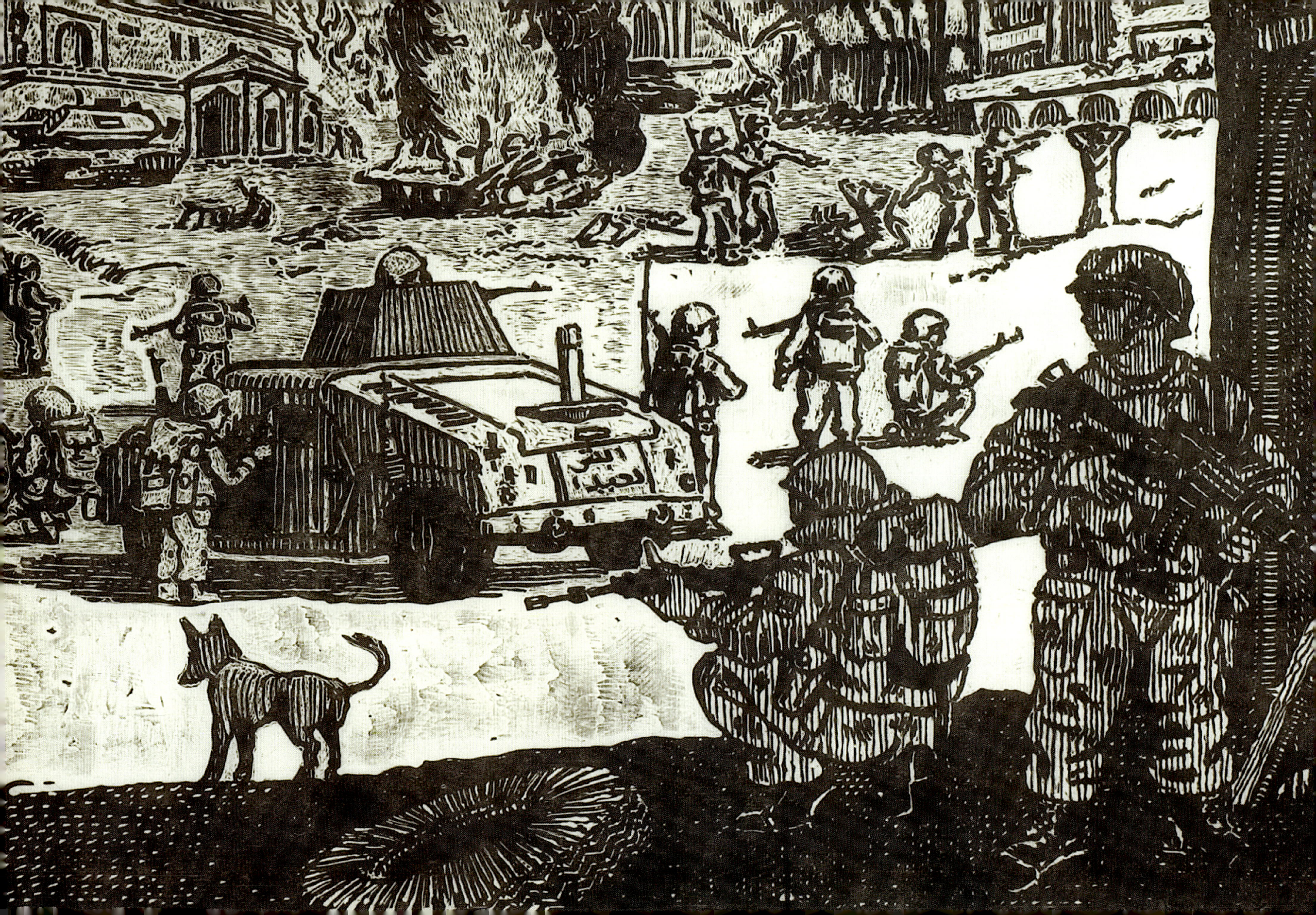

Contents

The Depravities of War

AN EXHIBITION OF FIFTEEN MONUMENTAL WOODCUTS BY SANDOW BIRK
PUBLISHED BY HUIPRESS, HUI NOʻEAU VISUAL ARTS CENTER, MAKAWAO, HAWAIʻI.

Exhibition Schedule

Catharine Clark Gallery, San Francisco, California
September 8 – October 20, 2007

University Art Museum
College of the Arts, California State University, Long Beach, California
November 8 – December 16, 2007

Alfred C. Glassell Jr. Exhibition Gallery, Shaw Center for the Arts
Louisiana State University School of Art, Baton Rouge, Louisiana
January 19 – February 17, 2008

Second Street Gallery, Charlottesville, Virginia
March 7 – April 12, 2008

Katzen Arts Center, American University Museum, Washington, DC
September 2 – October 26, 2008

In Gratitude

It would be fittingly ironic to say that more planning went into this project than into the invasion that it chronicles, but it was actually equally spontaneous, although perhaps less optimistic. What started as a vague idea – a body of work based on Jacques Callot's timeless and somewhat forgotten series of etchings – grew into this enormous project due essentially to the inspiration of Elyse Pignolet and the enthusiasm and dedication of Paul Mullowney and HuiPress.

Elyse has been involved with the project since its conceptual beginnings and it was her insight to take Callot's tiny etchings and expand them to heroic proportions. Paul Mullowney and his limitless enthusiasm and technical expertise made that nearly preposterous idea become feasible, and the resources of Hui No'eau Visual Arts Center made it a reality.

A project of this scope would never have been possible without the efforts of many, and Paul enlisted the assistance of several artists who worked tediously long hours cutting the woodblocks and adding their personal touches. No amount of thanks is sufficient to Casey Neumann, Katherine Godwin, Samuel Carr-Prindle, and Nichol Markowitz for their partnership in the project, for their hard work, for their talents and skills, for their unselfishness, and for their humor.

Greg Escalante was called into the project late and connected it to those at Grand Central Art Center. Andrea Harris-McGee and her relentless energy and experience were crucial, and there is no way I can thank either of them as much as they deserve.

Maui is a remote and idyllic island, and yet the repercussions of a distant war are still able to touch it. The military plays a large part in the state's economy and it has sent its sons and daughters around the globe to be tragically involved in the present conflict as, sadly, has the rest of the nation. If war is eternal – Hemingway has called it one of the great themes of man, along with love and death – it is also eternally lamentable and horrendous, no less so than in our country today, when our nation is in the midst of a war perhaps more horrible for un-necessity. It seems especially poignant that this project was realized in Maui, and that was possible only due to HuiPress and all of those involved in it. Thank you all.

Sandow Birk
Los Angeles, May 2007

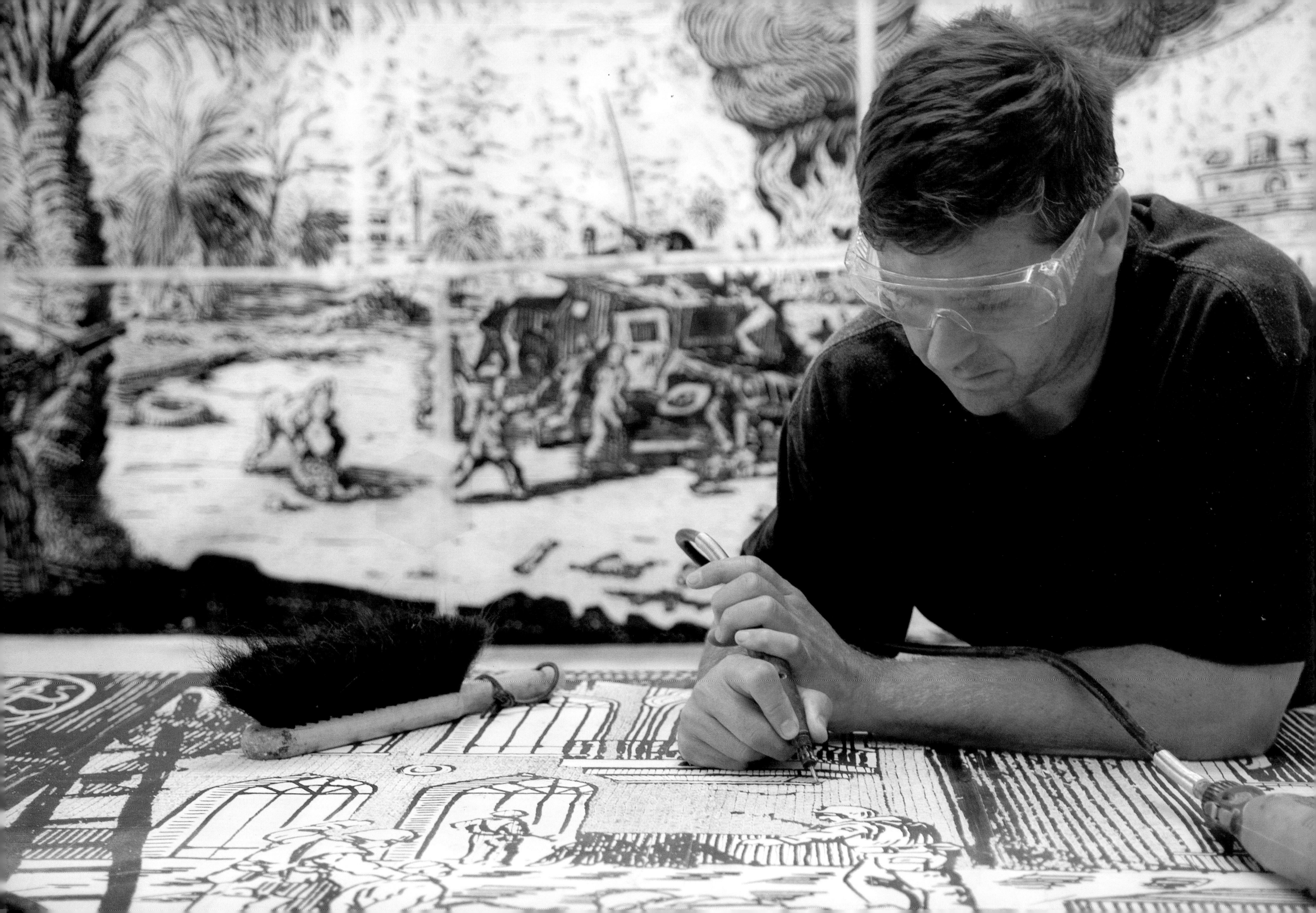

Terms of Engagement

by Darius A. Spieth, Ph.D., Assistant Professor of Art History, Louisiana State University

"To go by what the big shots say, they are waging war for almighty God and in the name of everything that's good and lovely. But look closer, they ain't so silly, they are waging it for what they can gain. Else little folk like me wouldn't be in it at all."

– Mother Courage in Bertolt Brecht's play *Mother Courage and Her Children: A Chronicle of the Thirty Years' War* (1939/1941)[1]

The prints and paintings comprised in Sandow Birk's *The Depravities of War* series stand in a time-honored iconographic tradition of Western art. Since the seventeenth century, artists have never tired of visually exploring the inequities of warfare, highlighting its degrading impact on the human condition with increasing urgency as the cataclysmic events of the nineteenth and twentieth centuries unfolded. Of course, the last hundred years have been sadly rich in occasions for artists to explore antimilitarist and pacifist material. In fact, the whole avant-garde tradition, from Dadaism, Surrealism, and Germany's "New Objectivity" to Picasso's *Guernica* and the artistic sympathizers with the peace movement of the late 1960s, would not have been conceivable without the experience of two world wars and an ensuing "Cold War" with its minor "hot" theaters scattered across Asia, Africa, and South America.[2] The fundamental cultural pessimism of the avant-garde owes much to the first experiments with biological and chemical weapons during World War I and to the realization in the wake of World War II that mankind, for the first time in its history, had attained the means to exterminate itself through nuclear warfare. Artists reacted to these developments with positions that have ranged from deliberate ridicule of the social classes, mostly the bourgeoisie, whose complacency was equated with complicity (Dadaism), to a nihilistic withdrawal (Surrealism) or an affirmation of existentialist autonomy (Abstract Expressionism).

As a twenty-first-century artist, Sandow Birk is certainly conversant with the role of the avant-garde artist struggling as an engaged intellectual against war and the authoritarian structures that support it. However, in the fifteen large-scale woodcut prints that form the core of his *Depravities of War* series, he references a different and much earlier artistic tradition dealing with armed conflicts. Jacques Callot's suite of etchings included in *The Large Miseries of War* portfolio, first published in 1633, was inspired by the atrocities committed by the marauding armies that ravaged much of Europe during the Thirty Years' War between 1618 and 1648.[3] But whereas the format, technique, and many of the themes espoused in Birk's *Depravities of War* make these prints worthy epigones of Callot's work, much of the specific iconography is excerpted from the media coverage of the ongoing war in Iraq. Although Birk mostly avoids direct references, it is obvious to the astute observer that his *Depravities of War* is a deliberate attempt to reinterpret Callot in terms of the events that have occurred in Iraq and the U.S. since the beginning of "Operation Iraqi Freedom" in 2003. Despite such historical specificities, the message of both Callot and Birk remains timeless: warfare follows its own immutable rules, from the cunning recruitment of soldiers and their training in the first stages of conflict to the logical progression of combat, destruction, spoliation, abuse, punishment, and death. It is the merit of Birk's series to highlight how little the basic functioning of these "terms of engagement" have changed over the last four hundred years, while leaving the formulation of a moral judgment on the events to the individual viewer.

Callot's War

Callot's *Large Miseries of War* was the product of two historical circumstances defining Europe in the early seventeenth century: the outbreak of a far-flung war triggered by religious and territorial controversies between Catholic and Protestant regions, combined with advances in military technology and professionalism.[4] Geographically, the artist was well positioned to observe the most gruesome aspects of this war from his native Lorraine region, situated near the Franco-German border area, where clashes between Catholic and Calvinist forces ravaged the lives of the peasant population in particular. Undoubtedly, the Lorraine counted amongst the most severely affected parts of Europe during the conflict.

The Thirty Years' War was the first war in Western history in which the casualty rate exceeded the ten-percent threshold, rising as high as 15.7%, while in previous wars from the twelfth to the sixteenth centuries only between 2.5% and 5.9% of the soldiers involved in the altercations met their end.[5] Most of this leap in mortality rate can be attributed to the increased availability of firearms, made possible by improvements in mass-manufacturing techniques. Thus, the musketeer became the most readily identifiable symbol of change in military technology on the battlefields of the Thirty Years' War.

Parallel to these technologically driven innovations, a new type of army emerged, one that was composed entirely of professional mercenaries and career soldiers. In combination, these two tendencies made for one of the deadliest wars ever seen to this date. Only in the twentieth century would there be a comparable increase in the efficiency of warfare, as the casualty rate for the century as a whole jumped to 38.9% in the wake of the two world wars.

More efficient military technology and training methods also meant a commensurate increase in destruction, cruelty, and loss of life among civilians, circumstances on which Callot dwelled extensively in his series of prints. The narrative framework for the eighteen etchings in the *Large Miseries of War* is established by the rendering of successive stages in the evolution of a generic war, which the seventeenth-century viewer, like the viewer of Birk's *Depravities* series, could not fail to associate with contemporary events. The set starts with *The Recruitment of Troops*, followed by *The Battle*.

Subsequently, five etchings deal with various crimes committed by soldiers: they pillage a humble inn and rob civilian travelers with as much fervor as they sack a large seigniorial country house (plate 5), a cloister, and a village. The plates illustrate the principle of "war feeding war," alluding to the marauding bands of soldiers, frequently left behind without pay, who took to pillaging and became the scourge of the countryside. A print depicting the *Discovery of Criminal Soldiers* provides the link to another subset of five etchings showing the punishment of the soldiers who misbehaved: they are tortured to death by strappado, hanged on a hanging tree (plate 11), executed by a firing squad, burned on a pyre, or broken on a wheel. But even those soldiers who survived the war and were not subject to such punishments face hardship, as two follow-up plates illustrate. The first one shows an assembly of sick and wounded soldiers in the courtyard of a hospital, the second one a small-town scene with veterans dying in the street. Callot's two concluding plates do not offer much consolation either: in the first scene, peasants take bloody revenge on the soldiers who had previously mistreated them so abominably. The final composition, however, shows the distribution of awards to good and obedient soldiers during an official reception.

Callot was not the only printmaker of his day to deal with the atrocities committed during the Thirty Years' War, but none of his contemporaries elaborated on the internal mechanisms of economic dependence, fear, intimidation, violence, and counter-violence that keep the clockwork of warfare going with such relentless immediacy.[6] What sets Callot's work apart is the universal validity of his artistic statement, which he attained by not depicting a specific war, but a generic one. The reason why Callot's imagery retains its power resides precisely in the fact that his war could be any war, anywhere, at any time.

Much of the modern-day effort at interpreting Callot's *Large Miseries of War* has focused on the question of whether he meant to condemn all warfare, in which case he would have to be regarded as the first antimilitarist artist in Western history.[7] The issue remains inconclusive, since some authors have maintained that such depravities were accepted by seventeenth-century societies as an inherent part of life, to be suffered with indifferent acceptance. Others have even gone so far as to impute to Callot a desire to amuse and charm the viewer with *guignols divertissants*, or "distracting puppetry."[8] Certainly, a present-day viewer would be tempted to interpret Callot's vision of war – and especially the culminating scene showing the distribution of awards – as a satirical, if not outright sarcastic statement. While such ironic intentions undoubtedly hold true for Sandow Birk's series and its postmodern lore of tongue-in-cheek historical referentiality, Callot may have been dead serious when extolling the rewards awaiting the virtuous soldiers who emerged unscathed from the ordeal.

Goya's Disasters

One has to wait until the early-nineteenth century to encounter an artistic statement unequivocally expressing genuine disgust with the atrocities of war. Francisco Goya was a Spanish painter and printmaker who lived through the tumultuous age of the French Revolution and its aftermath in the Napoleonic wars.[9] An *afrancesado*, or promoter of the Enlightenment ideas that arrived in backward Spain by way of France in the late-eighteenth century, Goya rose to a privileged position under the patronage of Spanish kings Charles III and Charles IV, who appointed him *Pintor del Rey* (Painter to the King, 1786) and *Pintor de Cámera* (Painter to the Royal Household, 1789). As the turn of the nineteenth century drew closer, Goya experienced a series of setbacks. In his personal life, he suffered from prolonged bouts of illness that left him deaf, but the darkening of his artistic vision owed even more to the political situation in Spain during the Napoleonic invasion and occupation of the country between 1808 and 1814.[10] Napoleon deposed the corrupt ruling family and installed his own brother, Joseph Bonaparte, on the Spanish throne. His administration then began to persecute recalcitrant members of the Catholic clergy who were unwilling to collaborate with the new secular and reform-minded regime. The Napoleonic policies in matters of faith and self-government poisoned relations with Spain's exceedingly pious population, which started a bloody guerrilla war, the first of its kind, pitching civilian insurgents against an organized occupation army. The very circumstance that the Spanish term *guerrilla* (literally, "little war"), which first gained currency at the time, continues to be used and understood in many languages other than Spanish is a tribute to the historical novelty of this type of "asymmetrical warfare" in the early-nineteenth century.

Goya could not help but feel ambiguous with respect to these events. As a reformer, he had supported the same Enlightenment ideals that took political shape in the French Revolution but subsequently went horribly awry with the wars, occupations, and decades of bloodshed that followed. The "dream of reason" produced monsters, as Goya himself was only too keenly aware. After Napoleon's fall and the reinstallation of the reactionary Bourbon monarchy under Ferdinand VII in Spain, Goya painted the *The Uprising of the Second of May 1808* and *The Executions of the Third of May 1808*. The two canvases were conceived as a tribute to the sacrifices of the common people, the *pueblo*, during the culmination of the native unrest in Madrid, when swift French military repression brought many of the insurgents before a French firing squad only twenty-four hours after the revolt was put down.

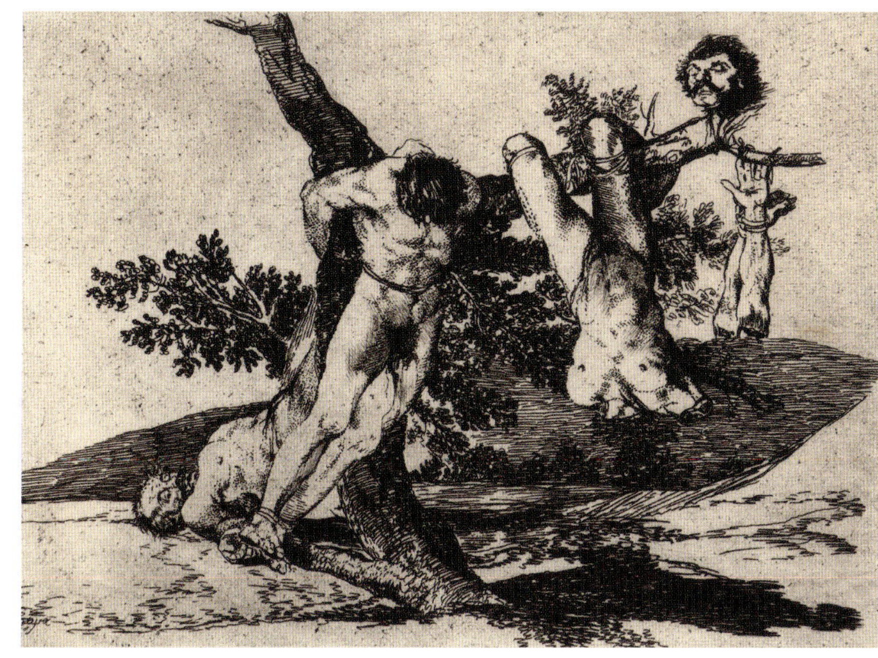

FIG. 1 Francisco de Goya, *Why?, What More Can One Do?, Great Deeds – Against the Dead*

Privately, Goya had long been pursuing a different vision of the events of the Peninsular War, one that was decidedly less heroic or patriotic than that espoused in his official paintings. The eighty-odd etchings that comprise his *Disasters of War* were produced during and after the conflict, but Goya never intended them for distribution during his lifetime, so the series went unpublished until 1863.[11] By contrast with Callot, there is no narrative or progression implied in *Los Desastres de la Guerra*. Rather, the scenes exist in isolation, with each print illuminating a different aspect of the panopticon of human cruelty and horror that unfolds. The earliest and largest subset of plates in the series is directly related to the guerrilla war fought against Napoleon's troops. This group of prints is followed by a smaller selection of some twenty subjects dealing with the Madrid famine of 1811-1812 and a similar number of *caprichos enfáticos*, "emphatic" or "striking" caprices, highlighting the repressive character of the reactionary politics that prevailed after the return of the Bourbons to the Spanish throne under Ferdinand VII.

Goya was not concerned with searching for reasons or with assigning moral blame in his prints, since he alternated images of French soldiers shooting or maiming Spanish men, women, and children with depictions of Spanish insurgents slaughtering wounded French soldiers who have already fallen to the ground (*With or without Reason, The Same Thing*). His perspective is always that of the victims of war, whether he is portraying the rape of a Spanish woman by a French soldier in *They Do not Want to* or mass execution scenes of bound and blindfolded insurgents facing a French firing squad in *And It Can't Be Helped*, the print that eventually influenced the compositional choices Goya made in his famous *Third of May* painting. The senselessness of violence is another central theme of the series: prisoners of war are tortured for amusement before being put to death, and even after the executions their bodies are dismembered and their severed extremities ostentatiously displayed (*Why?, What More Can One Do?, Great Deeds – Against the Dead* (fig. 1), among many similar examples).

Compared to Callot, there is certainly a greater psychological intensity implied by these works, owing to the fact that Goya was driven by unambiguously antimilitarist sentiments. This effect was achieved by reducing the number of figures per print and liberating them from Callot's antlike anonymity, thereby allowing for a more nuanced depiction of human emotions. In fact, Goya is believed to have known and studied Callot's *The Miseries of War*.[12] Like Callot, he was concerned with identifying the inner logic of war and describing the vicious circle of violence and revenge that it fuels. Nevertheless, as far as the actual compositions in the *Disasters of War* are concerned, Goya owed next to nothing to Callot, since he insisted that his prints be unedited eyewitness accounts. As he titled one of the most haunting of them, *Yo lo vi!* – "I saw it!"

Birk's Vision

Birk admires the work of Callot, but in spirit he is closer to Goya, whose critical position against war and referential attitude toward Callot he adopts as his own. He thus consciously continues the tradition of war prints begun by the former and perpetuated by the latter. His indebtedness to Callot is already obvious from the frontispiece featuring the shot-up, cubical building of a mosque (plate 19), whose silhouette mimics in no uncertain terms the shape of the ornamental tablet on the colophon opening the *Large Miseries of War* (plate 1). The Orientalizing background details of Birk's composition set the tone for the series as a whole: there are veiled women and praying or surrendering (the ambiguity appears deliberate) Arabic men, simultaneously protected and threatened by armed members of the Western military. The scene stands out against the stark silhouette of a generic Middle-Eastern town ravaged, as suggested by a smoke-filled sky, by terrorist attacks or insurgencies.

Obsession (plate 20), the opening woodcut of the set, depicts a scene closer to home. The composition follows conceptually Callot's *The Recruitment of Troops* etching (plate 2), except that the present-day recruits are not lured by alcohol, trumpet sounds, and colorful uniforms, as was the custom in the seventeenth century, but by the promise of "free college," an offer announced prominently on the banner of the army recruitment table to the right. In the middle-ground, new recruits bid a tearful good-bye to friends and family as they depart in marching order against a signage-studded American sky. In the far distance, on the left side of the composition, airplanes plunge into two modern high-rises reminiscent of New York's Twin Towers, thereby alluding to the 9/11 terrorist attacks that provided the political backdrop for the American invasion of Iraq. The next scene (plate 21) already reveals the martial reality of combat. Troops are trained as parachutists or as armed combatants. Once the training is complete, they board a fleet of military aircraft bound for an as-yet-unknown destination.

With *Invasion* (plate 22), the associations with media images from the beginning of the Iraq war loom stronger in the viewer's mind. The apocalyptic scenery features a desert plain replete with burning oil fields in the distance and a tank ablaze amidst oil-stained human corpses strewn about in the left foreground. As battleship helicopters hover on the horizon, an armada of intact tanks races across the plain below. Birk sketches a narrative scenario that is based on the same seemingly inevitable rules that define Callot's and Goya's imagery. The prints entitled *Incursion, Destruction, Desecration, Occupation,* and *Insurrection* (plates 23–27) provide snapshots from the subsequent stages of the Middle-Eastern conquest. In *Occupation,* Western soldiers have taken over the central square of a town after what appears to have been heavy fighting. One military vehicle and several buildings have been set ablaze. As a reminder of Callot's influence, the house on the right margin of the composition references the *Plundering and Burning a Village* plate (plate 7) from *The Miseries of War,* but hybridizes the structure with Arabic architectural elements. A more urban setting is featured in *Incursion,* where the invading troops storm a larger, walled-in compound. The moral dilemma of the war takes its course, as increasing numbers of prisoners are being captured. The twilight of the conflict is reached in *Destruction,* where Western soldiers have stormed and now are about to loot a mosque in which insurgents might have hidden. In a pendant print entitled *Desecration,* the interior of a mosque is being searched by the intruders. Both subjects are based on photographic footage that appeared in the *Los Angeles Times* of American troops relaxing inside the ruined mosque at Fallujah. However, the iconography reminds the viewer equally of such well-publicized events as the looting of the National Museum in Baghdad, the siege of the Imam Ali Mosque during the battle of Najaf, or the Al-Askariya shrine bombing, which infamously destroyed the golden dome of this Shiite mosque in Samarra.[13] Birk's compositions take their cue from Callot's *Destruction of a Convent* (plate 6) and *Plundering a Large Farmhouse* (plate 5), respectively, which feature exterior and interior views of plunder during the Thirty Years' War. The price to pay for such reckless activities finally becomes obvious in *Insurrection,* where insurgents have attacked a convoy of Humvees, and military rescue forces scramble to save the latest victims of the conflict. The exposure of the Abu Ghraib prison scandal and Saddam Hussein's butchered execution have colored the public perception of the aftermath of the Iraqi conquest. Not surprisingly, several prints, *Detention, Degradation, Humiliation,* and *Execution* (plates 28–30, 32), deal with the treatment of prisoners of war during the Iraq conflict. One's familiarity with this shocking imagery and its contemporary political context should not obscure the fact that condemnation of the inhumane treatment of the conquered enemy was already key to Callot's and Goya's pictorial messages.

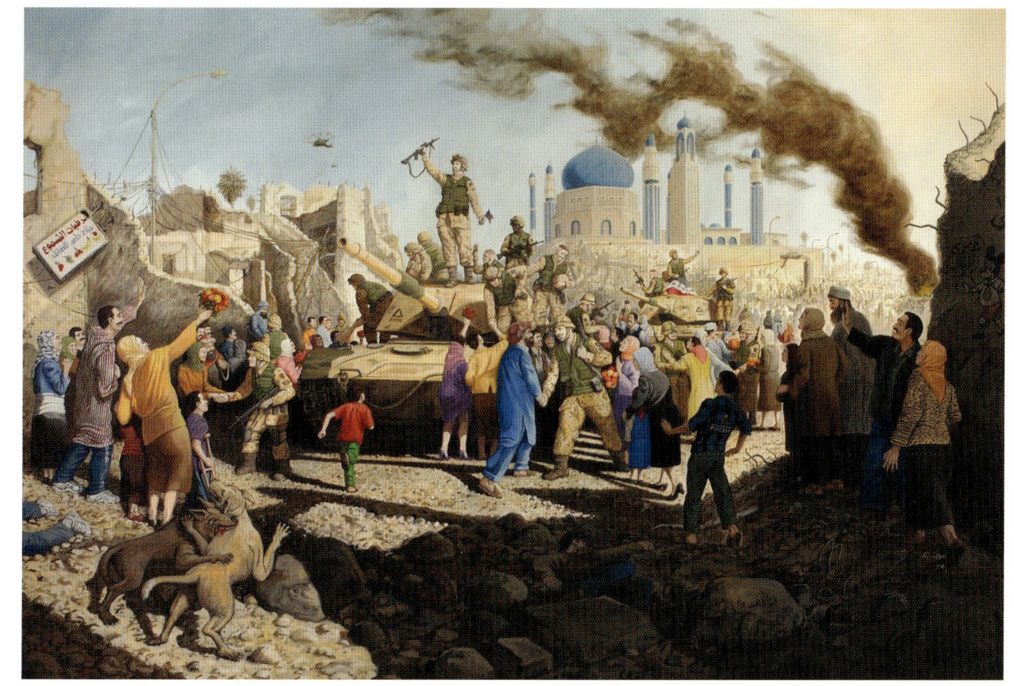

FIG. 2 Sandow Birk, *The Liberation of Baghdad*

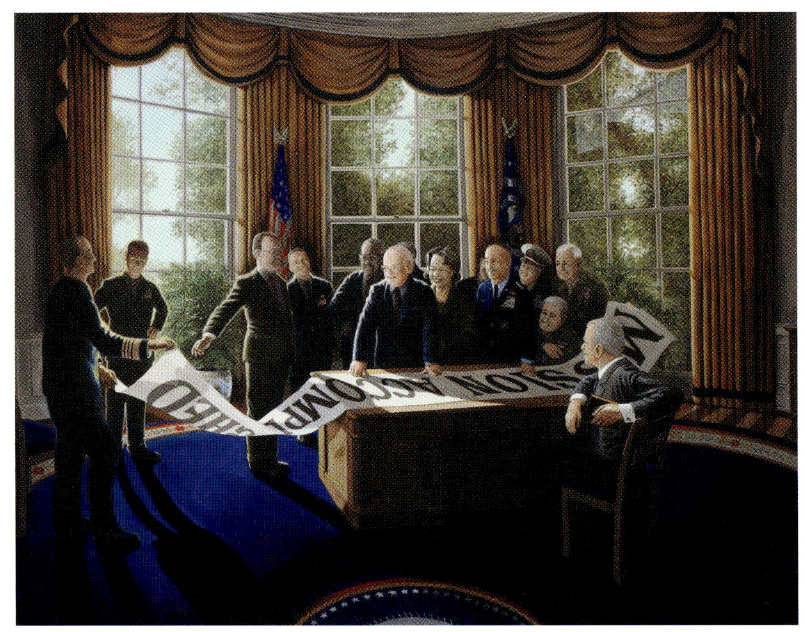

FIG. 3 Sandow Birk, *Secretary of State Donald Rumsfeld Presenting His Plan for the Invasion of Iraq*

Moreover, Birk could draw from his own take on prison iconography, previously developed while working on his *Prisonation* project, a series of paintings completed in 2001 that critically commented on the social and human costs of mushrooming incarceration rates in the California correctional system.[14] *Detention*, therefore, presents the viewer with one of the inevitable outcomes of occupation and the ensuing insurrection: suspects are held at gunpoint by the military, marched to trucks, and driven away. *Degradation* and *Humiliation* are scenes from inside a prison compound, incorporating details from the photographic records that revealed the Abu Ghraib prison scandal. The former woodcut shows an outdoor courtyard of a jail, where prisoners are photographed, shackled, stripped naked (except for their hoods), held in cages, and taunted by female prison guards – a tongue-in-cheek reference to the infamous misdeeds of Lynndie England in the said prison complex.[15] Even the prison tower in the background faithfully reproduces the genuine structure overlooking the Abu Ghraib facility. A true theater of horrors and torture, *Humiliation* is an indoor scene populated by the same cast of largely naked and hooded prisoners and their guards. Some of the inmates are threatened by attack dogs, while others are stacked to form human pyramids, tied to the second-floor gallery, or wired up and left standing with outstretched arms on a pedestal. In *Execution*, the administration of violence has finally been turned over to native hands. The iconography apparently references Callot's famous *The Hanging Tree* (plate 11), but in Birk's version only a single individual is being hung to the amusement and edification of the masses assembled below the gallows. A single soldier to the far left is making a (clandestine?) podcast of the execution, which will assure the timely dissemination of the gruesome imagery by electronic means.

Another two woodcuts deal with the aftermath of the war chronicled in the previous prints. *Repercussion* (plate 33) features the skyline of an American city in the background. The foreground, however, is populated by maimed veterans seeking treatment in an army hospital complex. Standing in line to be admitted to the facility, the veterans, on their crutches and in their wheelchairs, function as an eerie reminder not only of Callot's analogous plate *The Hospital* (plate 15), depicting the sick and wounded seeking treatment in the courtyard of a Baroque hospital, but also of the recent scandal involving the Walter Reed Army Medical Center, where wounded soldiers returning from Iraq complained about bug-infested, substandard treatment facilities and an inordinate amount of red tape.[16] The conflict's logic comes to a close in *Investigation* (plate 31), which evokes the compositional formula established by Callot's *Distribution of Rewards* (plate 18), but gives a very different meaning to the outcome.

Whereas in the *Large Miseries of War* the good soldiers are being rewarded, in Birk's version of the events a senate hearing on what went wrong in going to war provides a legitimating fig leaf of bureaucratic protocol. The anticlimactic conclusion of the series highlights the fact that there were no heroes to be found in this war.

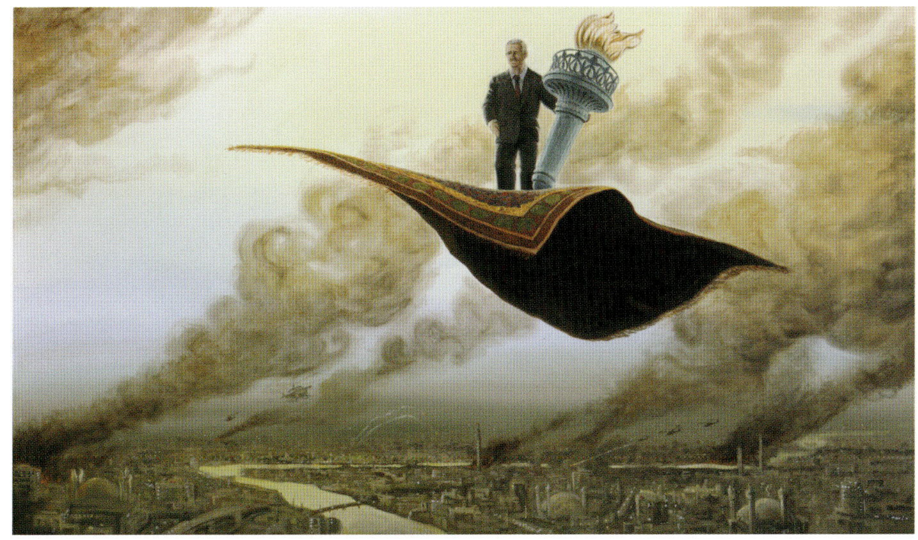

FIG. 4 Sandow Birk, *The President's Dream*

Indeed, to find explicit pointers for the historical grounding of Birk's iconography, one has to turn to the more limited number of oil paintings that are conceived as companion pieces to the *Depravities of War* woodcuts. In *The Liberation of Baghdad* (fig. 2) the artist envisioned an idealized closure of the conflict, one in which the native civilian population greets the American liberators with flowers, handshakes, and gestures of fraternization, while remaining completely oblivious to the demolished urban infrastructure in which they are now forced to live. Although today the image comes across as an ironic commentary in light of subsequent events in Iraq, Birk attempted in this canvas to give visual form to the Bush administration's publicly announced expectation of what the native welcome to an American invasion would look like. The precedent for such imagery (and its concomitant wishful thinking) could be found in the many black-and-white pictures of the American liberation of France after WWII. However, as no one can any longer deny, Baghdad in April 2003 was not Paris in 1945.

Ironic strategies also define the content of *Donald Rumsfeld Presenting His Plan for the Invasion of Iraq* and *The President's Dream* (figs. 3-4). The former composition grants us a view into the Oval Office while Secretary of Defense Donald Rumsfeld and his leading generals introduce a Bible-clutching president to the "Mission Accomplished" banner, later to be hung as a backdrop from the bridge of the USS *Abraham Lincoln* during Bush's declaration of the "end of major combat activities" in Iraq on May 1, 2003. True to the best tradition of nineteenth-century academic group portraits, the composition reflects Birk's research into who were the movers and shakers behind the decision to go to war, as all of the members of the military are individualized and thus readily identifiable. *The President's Dream* is a more fantastic and humorous scene featuring President George W. Bush holding an oversized torch temporarily "borrowed" from the Statue of Liberty, as he flies on a stealth-bomber-shaped Oriental carpet over war-torn Baghdad. The painting begs the question of whether he will ever be able to realize his dream of bringing democracy to the devastated country.

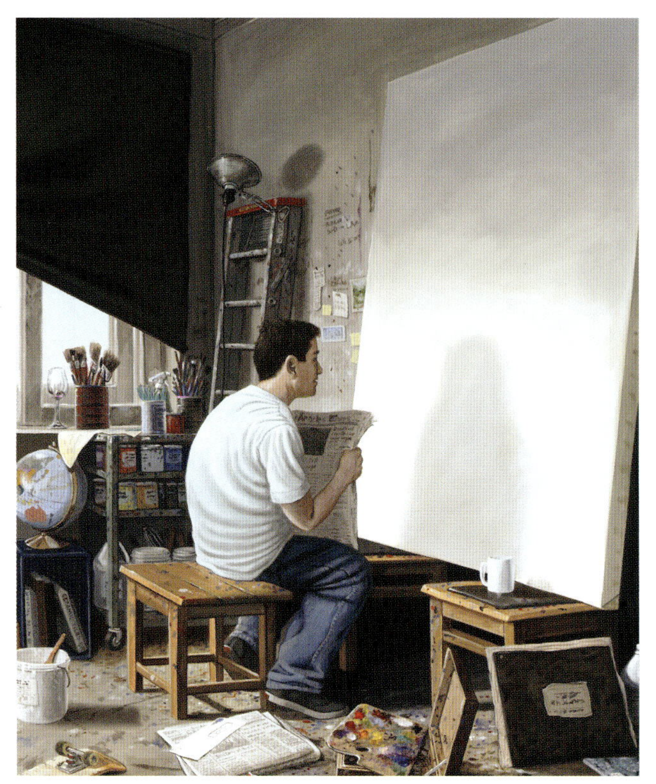

FIG. 5 Sandow Birk, *In Days of War*

Perhaps the most thought-provoking painting in the series is *In Days of War* (fig. 5). The work depicts a scene from the artist's California studio, where he is facing a newly stretched, white canvas while reading the headlines of a newspaper conveying the latest news about the war in Iraq. Contrary to what the title suggests, it is an intimate and peaceful scene, so very different from the violent visions previously discussed. Yet, it is an important and contemplative moment that is depicted here, raising questions about the role of the artist in contemporary political and social discourse. Birk asks us what has become of the traditional role of the artist as an independent moral conscience of society. Can artists afford to stay silent when faced with events so fundamental as to threaten world peace?

Birk's *Depravities of War* arrives at a moment when popular support for the war in Iraq is at an all-time low. Yet, the works in the series should not be interpreted as political commentaries so much as universal statements about the nature of warfare and violence. They raise the question of whether war can still be regarded as an acceptable means to resolve political differences in the twenty-first century. The motto of the nineteenth-century German theoretician of war, Carl von Clausewitz, that war is "merely a continuation of politics by other means"[17] – a rationale to which the Bush administration and its supporters implicitly subscribed when making the decision to go to war in Iraq – will have to be critically evaluated in an age when a steadily growing world population competes over natural resources just as steadily diminishing. Failure to resolve global conflicts peacefully is likely to result in more disastrous outcomes than ever before in human history – consequences that cannot but negatively affect the prosperity and quality of life of *all* parties involved. Sandow Birk's art is a timely reminder of this inconvenient truth.

1 Bertolt Brecht, "Mutter Courage und ihre Kinder. Eine Chronik aus dem Dreißigjährigen Krieg," in *Werke: Berliner und Frankfurter Ausgabe*, eds. Werner Hecht, Jan Knopf, Werner Mittenzwei, et al. (Berlin and Frankfurt: Aufbau-Verlag, Suhrkamp Verlag, 1989), 6:31-32. English translation in *Bertolt Brecht: The Good Person of Szechwan, Mother Courage and Her Children, Fear and Misery of the Third Reich*, tr. John Willett (New York: Arcade Publishing, 1993), 121.

2 See for instance Robert Hughes, *The Shock of the New*, rev. ed. (New York: Alfred A. Knopf, 1991), 57-111, 212-364; Antoine Compagnon, *The Five Paradoxes of Modernity*, tr. Franklin Philip (New York: Columbia University Press, 1994), 57-111.

3 The *Large Miseries of War* was preceded by the *Small Miseries of War*, a less ambitious trial run of the series consisting of only six plates executed in smaller formats and dating from ca. 1632, which never attained the iconic fame of the larger set. On the *Large Miseries of War* see for example Howard Daniel, *The World of Jacques Callot* (New York: Lear Publishers, 1948), 42-51; Francisco Goya, *The Disasters of War by Francisco Goya y Lucientes* (New York: Dover, 1967); Diane Wolfthal, "Jacques Callot's *Miseries of War*," in *Art Bulletin* 59, no. 2 (June 1977): 222-33; Paulette Choné, "Les Misères de la guerre, ou 'la vie du soldat': La force du droit," in *Jacques Callot, 1592-1635*, exh. cat. (Paris: Réunion des musées nationaux, 1992), 396-411; Linda C. Hults, *The Print in the Western World* (Madison: University of Wisconsin Press, 1996), 210-12.

4 On the history of the Thirty Years' War, see for example Cicely Veronica Wedgwood, *The Thirty Years' War* (London and New York: Methuen, 1981); *The Thirty Years' War*, ed. Geoffrey Parker, 2nd ed. (London and New York, 1997). On the Thirty Years' War in the Lorraine, see also Victor Lucien Tapié, *France in the Age of Louis XIII and Richelieu* (Cambridge and New York: Cambridge University Press, 1984).

5 Herbert Langner, *Thirty Years' War*, tr. C.S.V. Salt (New York: Hippocrene Books, 1980), 7-8.

6 For a spectrum of prints depicting the Thirty Years' War by artists other than Callot, see *1648: Krieg und Frieden in Europa*, eds. Klaus Bußmann und Heinz Schilling, exh. cat. (Münster and Osnabrück: Veranstaltungsgesellschaft 350 Jahre Westfälischer Friede, 1998), 155-82.

7 For a survey of modern attempts at interpreting Callot's war iconography, see Wolfthal, 224-25 and 232-33.

8 Pierre-Paul Plan, *Jacques Callot, maître graveur, 1593-1653* (Paris and Brussels: G. Van Oest & Cie, 1911), 18-19, 26-27.

9 On Goya's art and career, see for instance Gwyn A. Williams, *Goya and the Impossible Revolution* (London and New York: Pantheon, 1976); Fred Licht, *Goya* (New York and London: Abbeville Publishers, 2001).

10 On the Peninsular War in general, see Charles D. Esdaile, *The Peninsular War*, new ed. (New York and Houndmills: Palgrave Macmillan, 2003); David Gates, *The Spanish Ulcer: A History of the Peninsular War* (New York and London: Norton, 1986); Jean Thiry, *La guerre en Espagne* (Paris: Berger-Levrault, 1965).

11 On Goya's *Disasters of War*, see Francisco Goya, *The Disasters of War* (New York: Phaidon, 1937); *The Complete Etchings of Goya* (New York: Crown Publishers, 1943); Licht, 174-203; Hults, 412-17.

12 Licht, 193-94. Moreover, several recent publications and exhibitions have underscored that Goya's *Disasters of War* stand in the iconographic tradition of Callot's *Miseries of War*, a lineage continued by Otto Dix in the twentieth century and Birk in the twenty-first. See *Fatal Consequences: Callot, Goya, and the Horrors of War*, eds. Hilliard T. Goldfarb and Reva Wolf, exh. cat. (Hanover, NH: Hood Museum of Art, Dartmouth College, 1990); *Disasters of War: Callot, Goya, Dix*, eds. Antony Griffiths, Juliet Wilson Bareau, and John Willett, exh. cat. (Manchester: National Touring Exhibition and Hayward Gallery, 1998); *Jacques Callot, Francisco de Goya, Otto Dix: 3 Visiones de la Guerra*, exh cat. (Valencia: Fondación Bancaja, 2001).

13 On the looting of the Baghdad National Museum, see for instance John F. Burns, "Pillagers Strip Iraqi Museum of Its Treasure," in *New York Times* 152, no. 52,452 (April 13, 2003): A1, B3; on the siege and destruction of the Imam Ali Mosque in Najaf, see for example Alex Berenson, "After the Siege, a City of Ruins, Its Dead Rotting," in *New York Times* 153, no. 52,955 (August 28, 2004): A1, A7; on the Al-Askariya shrine bombing, see Marc Santora, "One Year Later, Golden Mosque Is Still in Ruins," in *New York Times* 156, no. 53,854 (February 13, 2007): A1, A9. On the destruction of shrines in general, see John F. Burns, "Iraq Government Calls for an End to Mosque Raids," in *New York Times* 154, no. 53,217 (May 17, 2005): A1, A10.

14 Darius A. Spieth, "The Prison in the Garden: Inside Sandow Birk's Topography of Incarceration," in *Incarcerated: Visions of California in the 21st Century*, exh. cat. (Santa Barbara, CA: Santa Barbara Contemporary Arts Forum, 2001), 7-15.

15 See for instance Ralph Blumenthal, "Sentencing Hearing Starts for G.I. Featured in Abu Ghraib Pictures," in *New York Times* 154, no. 53,204 (May 4, 2005): A14; Kate Zernike, "Behind Failed Abu Ghraib Plea, a Tangle of Bonds and Betrayals," in *New York Times* 154, no. 53,210 (May 10, 2005): A1, A13.

16 See for instance Michael Luo, "Soldiers Testify over Poor Care at Walter Reed," in *New York Times* 156, no. 53,875 (March 6, 2007): A1, A14.

17 Carl von Clausewitz, *Vom Kriege* (Bonn: Dümmler, 1951), 108. English translation in Carl von Clausewitz, *On War*, ed. and tr. Michael Howard and Peter Paret (Princeton: Princeton University Press, 1976), 87.

JACQUES CALLOT

The Miseries of War

Jacques Callot, *Miseries of War*

Suite of eighteen etchings made in 1633, approximately 3 1/4 x 7 1/4 inches each.

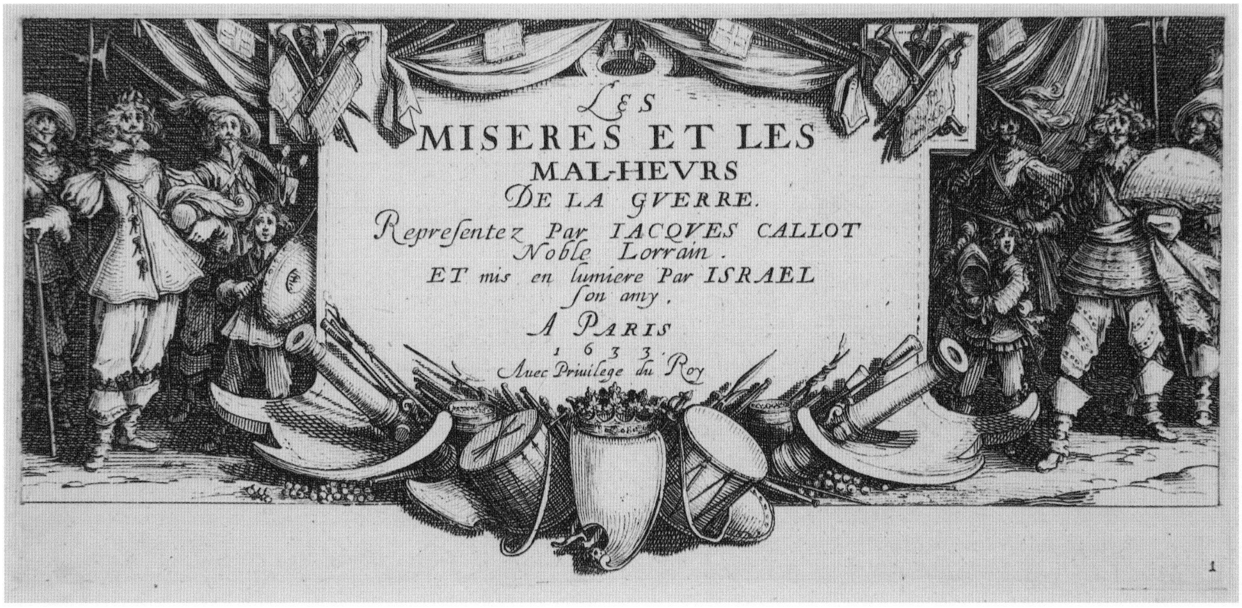

PLATE 1

Frontispiece

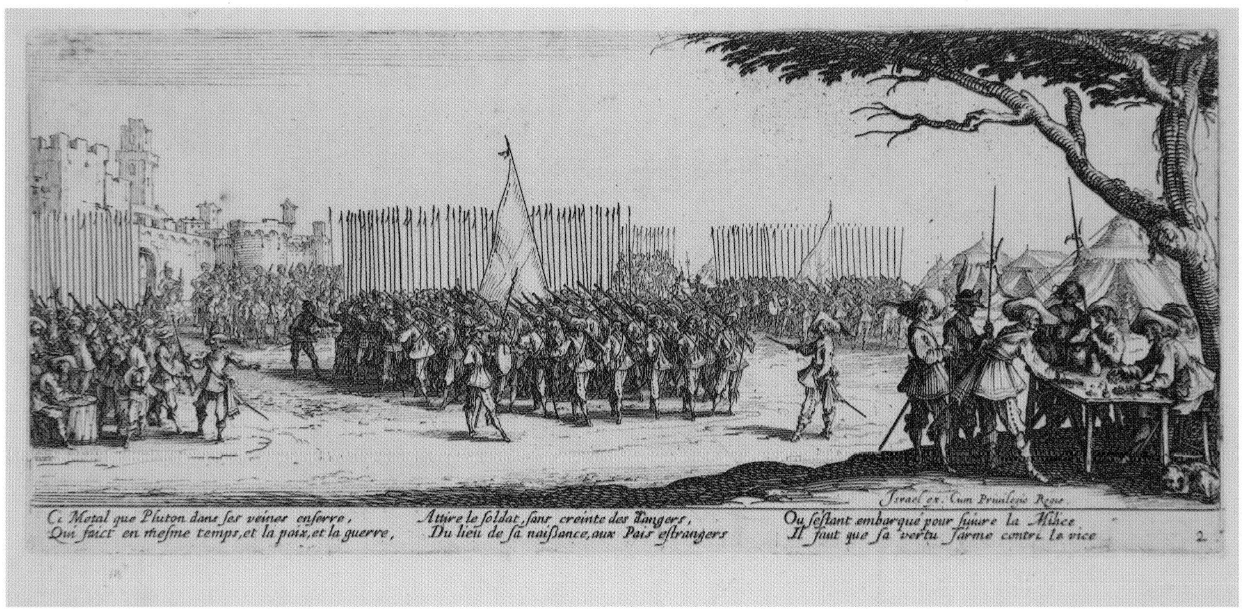

PLATE 2

The Recruitment of Troops

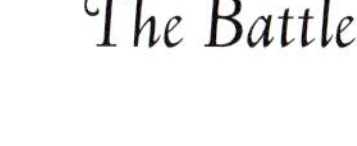

PLATE 3

The Battle

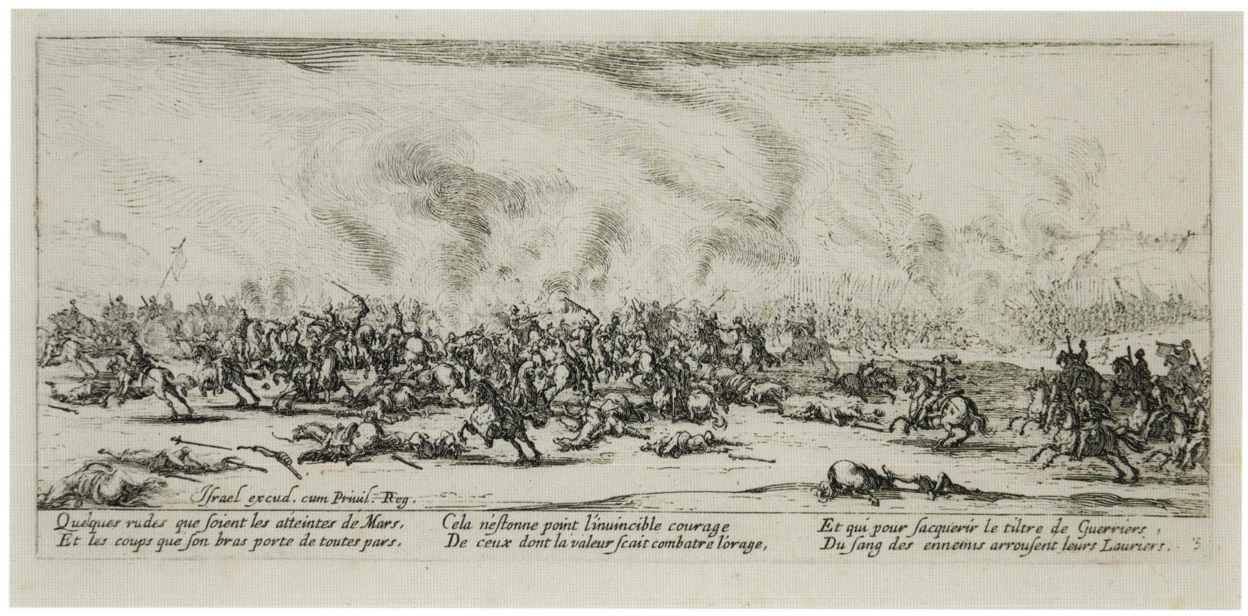

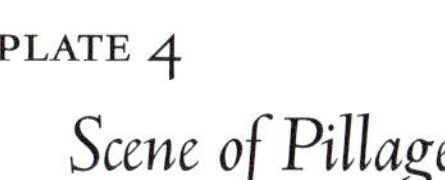

PLATE 4

Scene of Pillage

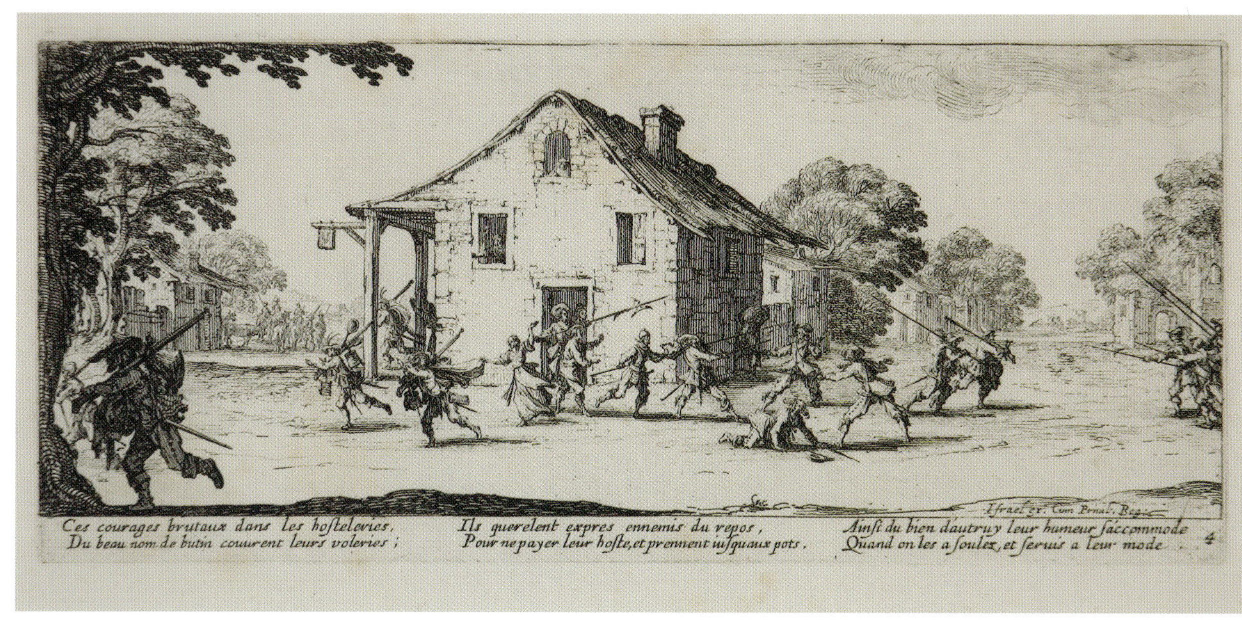

PLATE 5

Plundering a Large Farmhouse

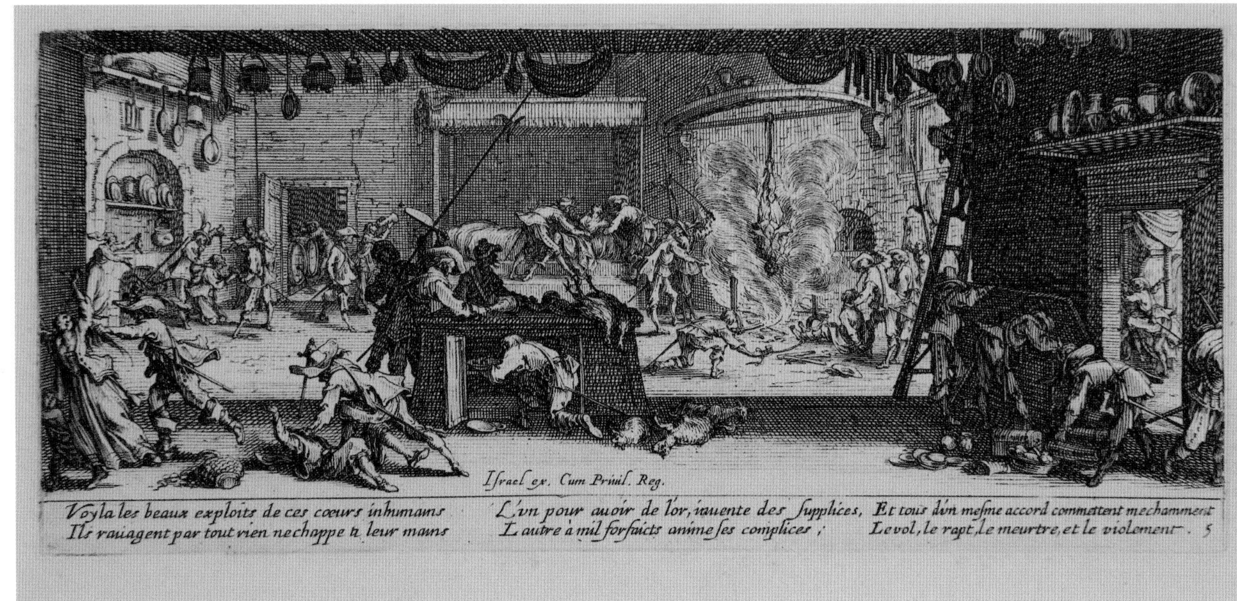

PLATE 6

Destruction of a Convent

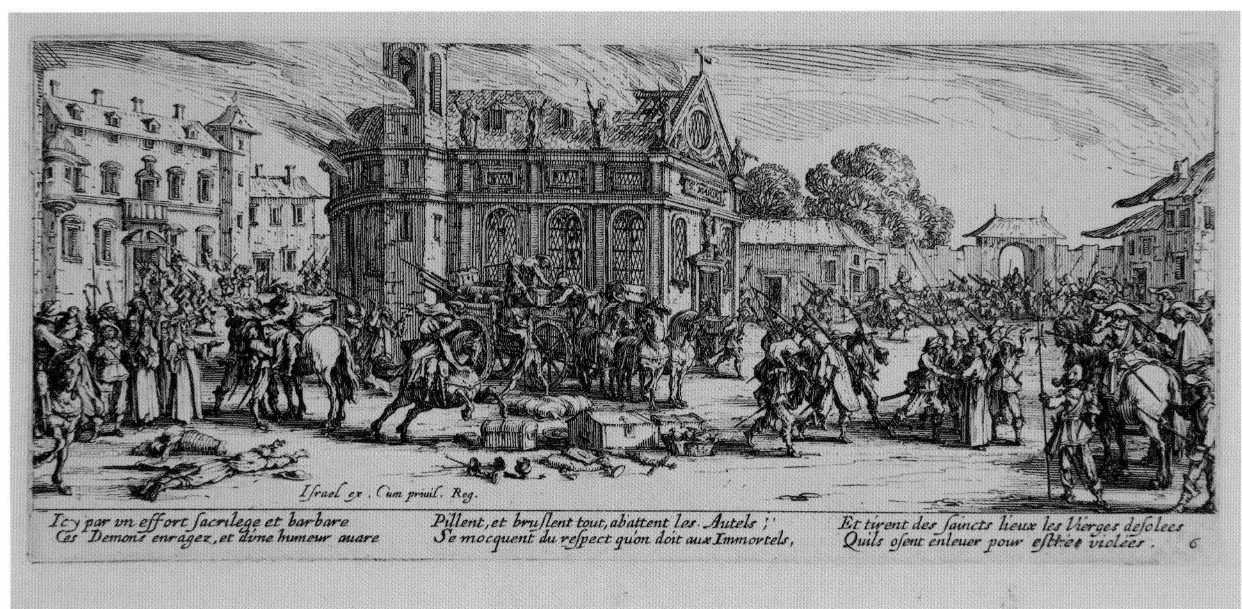

Israel ex. Cum Priuil. Reg.

Ceux que Mars entretient de ses actes meschans
Accommodent ainsi les pauures gens des champs

Ils les font prisonniers ils bruslent leurs villages,
Et sur le bestail mesme exercent des rauages,

Sans que la peur des Loix non plus que le deuoir.
Ny les pleurs et les cris les puissent esmouuoir. 7

PLATE 7

Plundering and Burning a Village

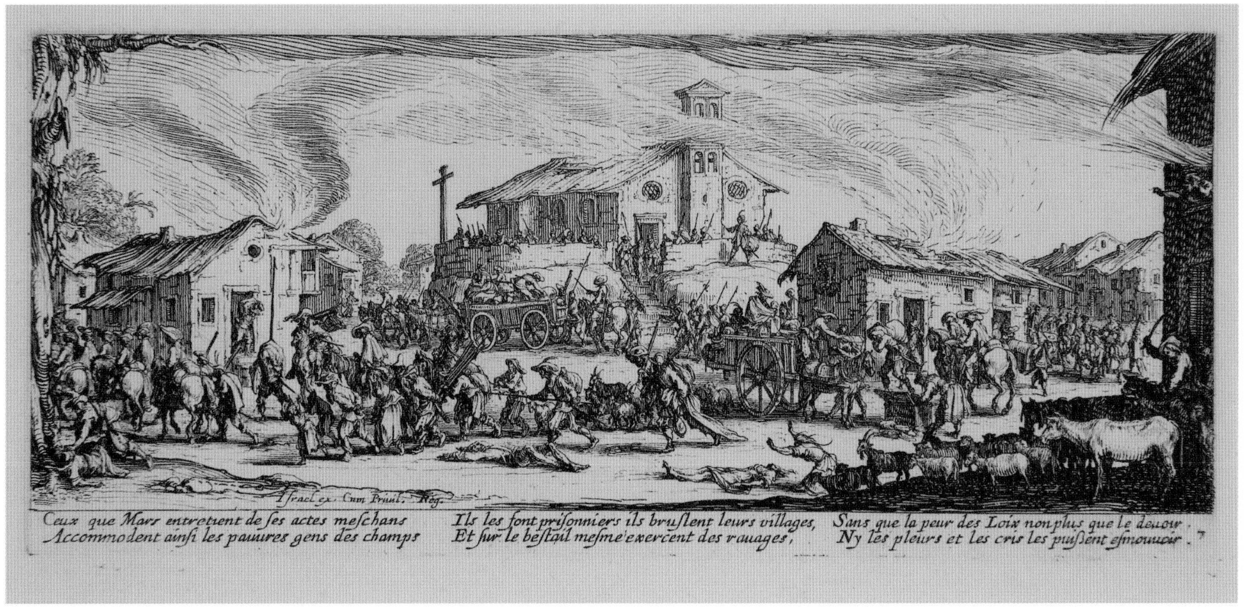

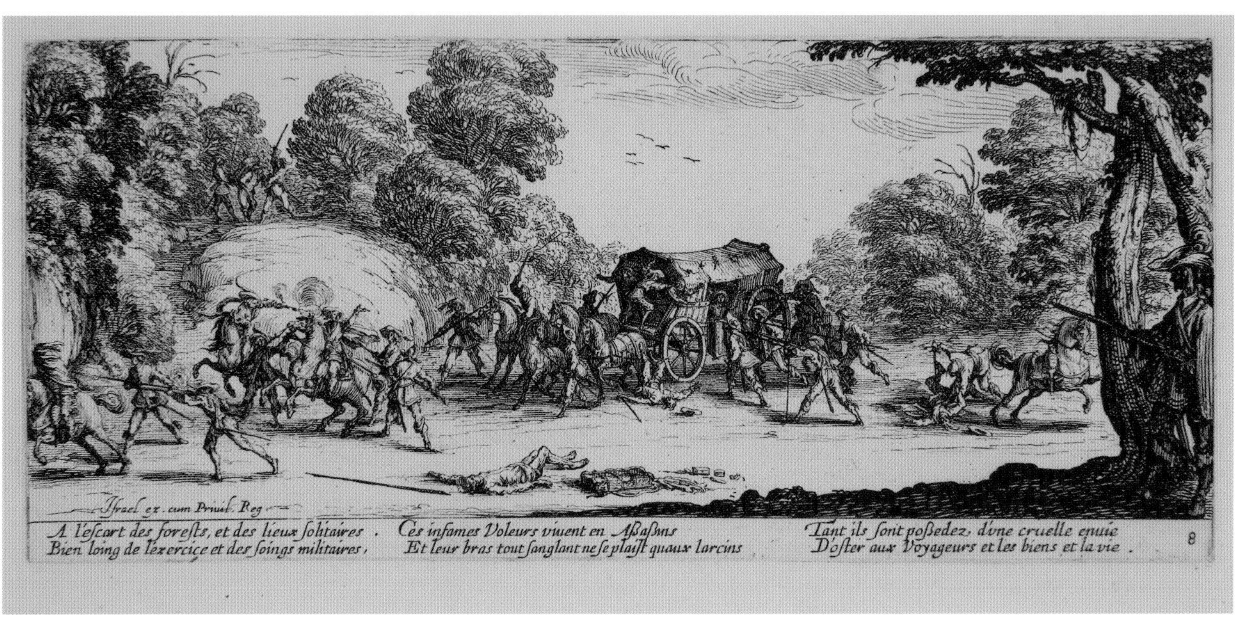

PLATE 8

Attack on a Coach

PLATE 9

Discovery of Criminal Soldiers

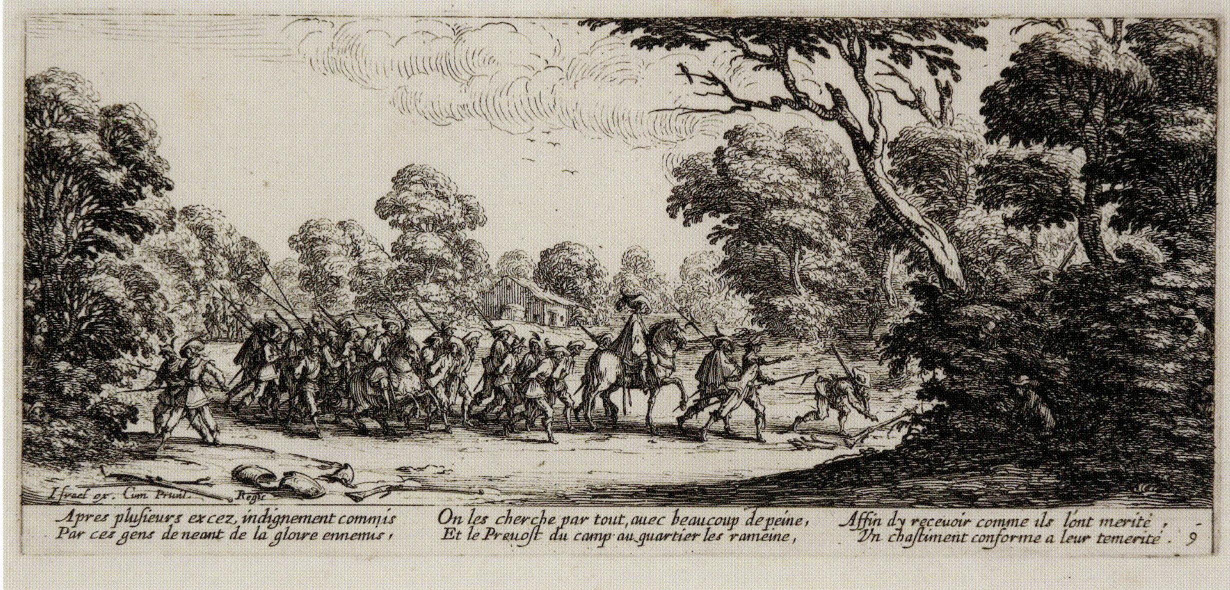

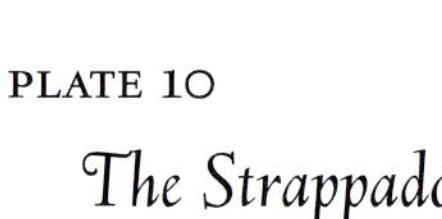

PLATE 10

The Strappado

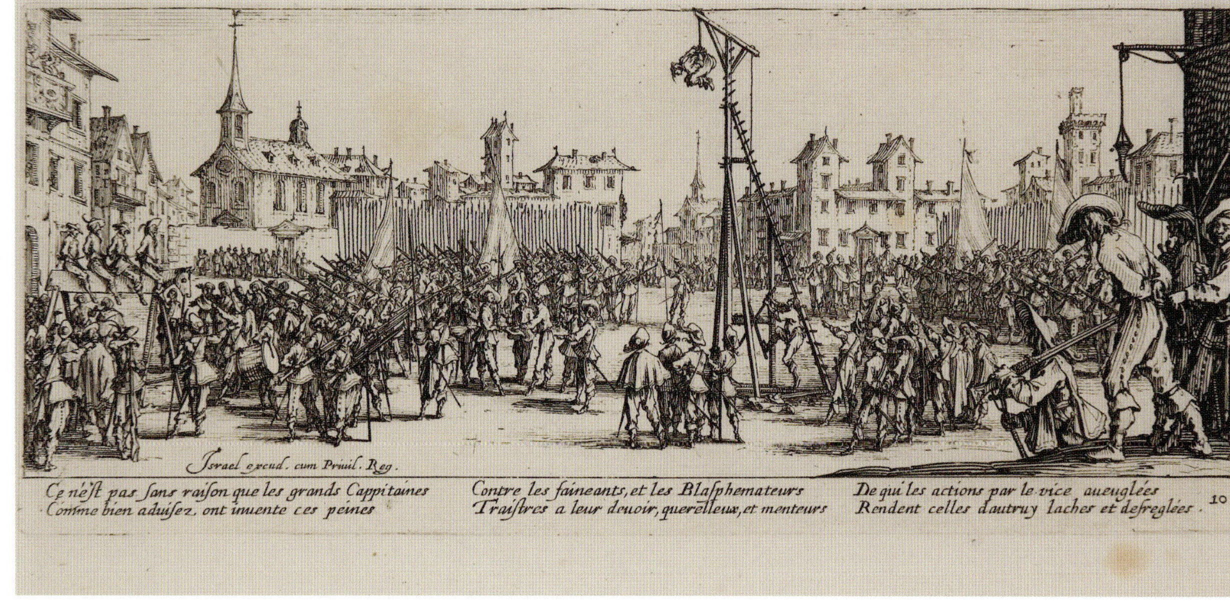

PLATE 11

The Hanging Tree

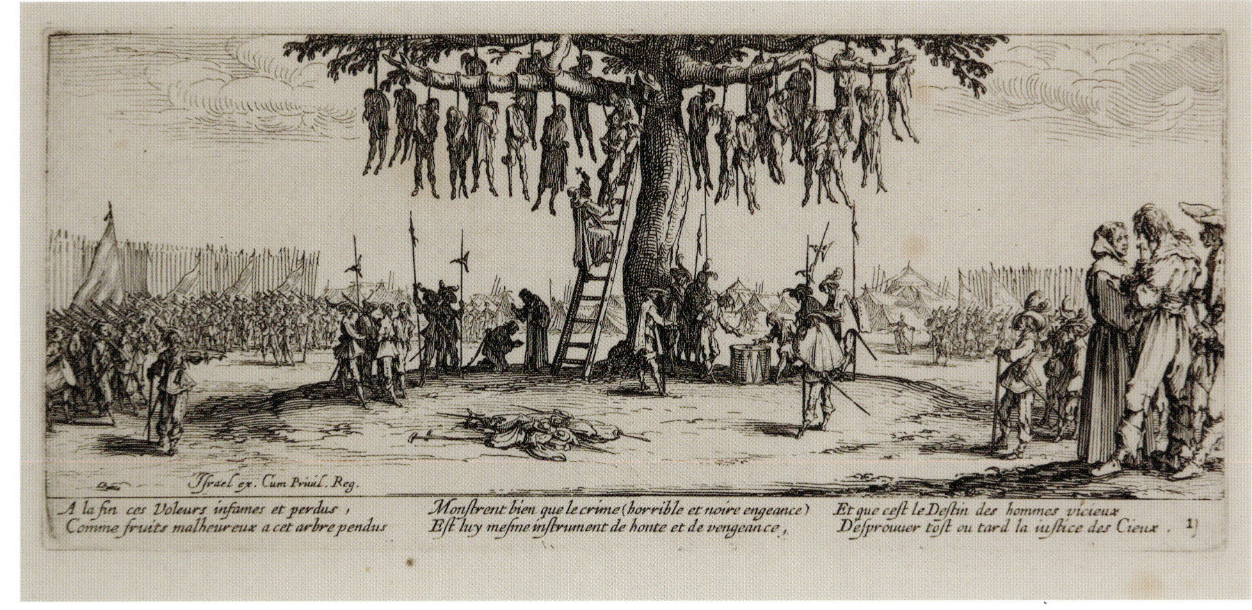

PLATE 12

The Firing Squad

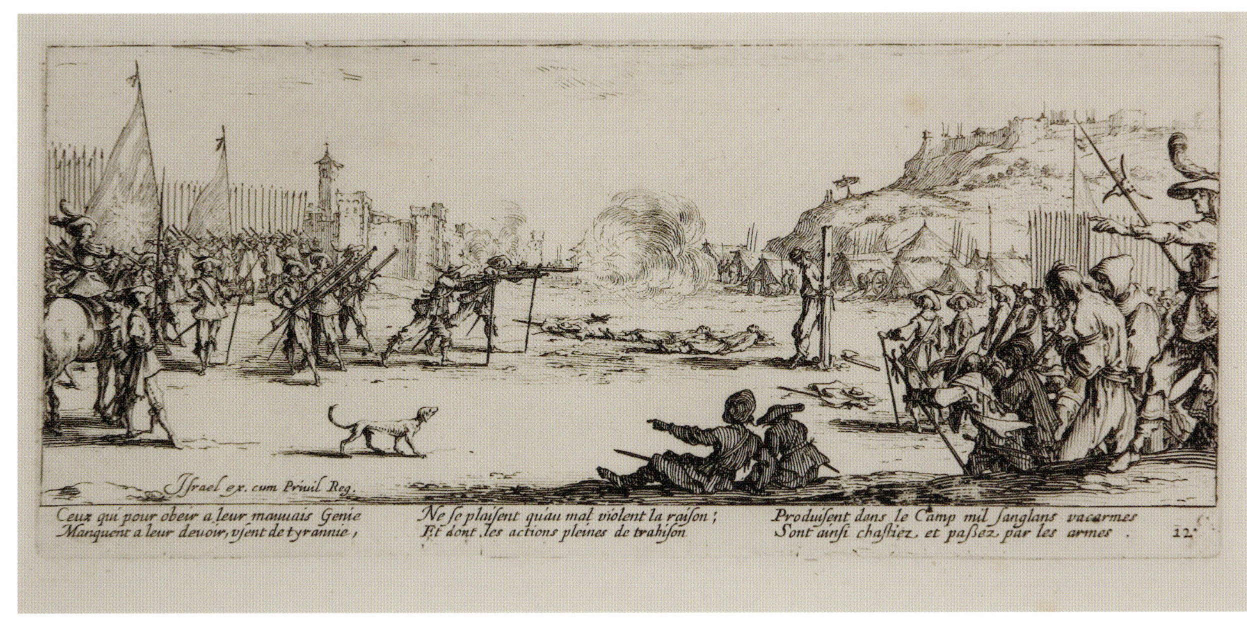

PLATE 13

The Stake

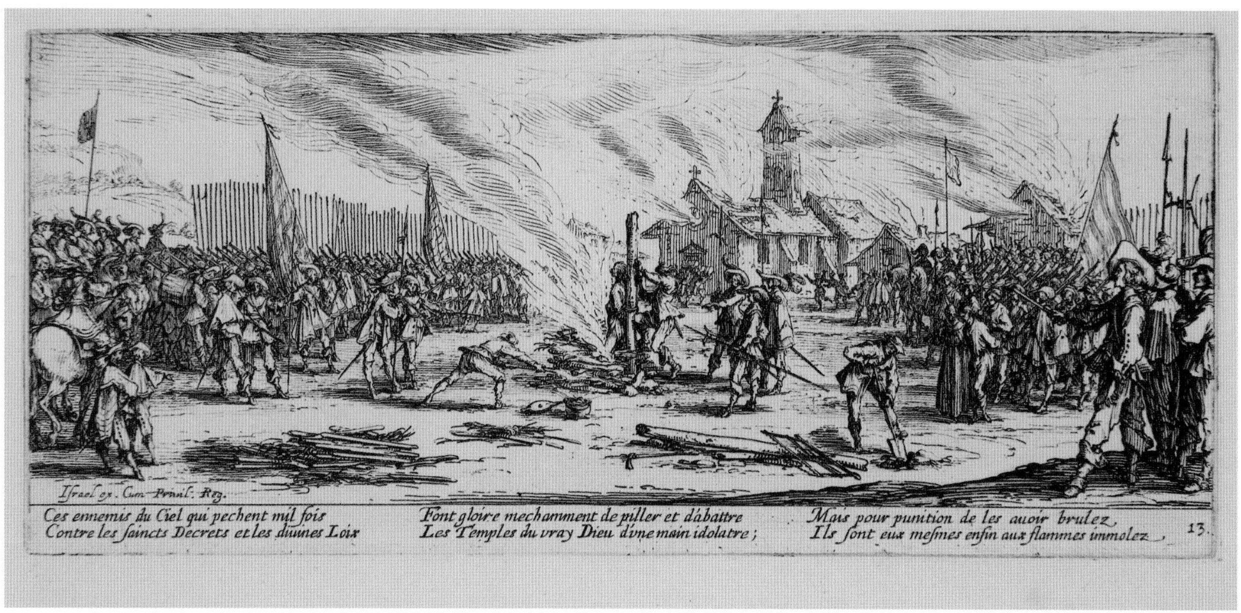

PLATE 14

The Wheel

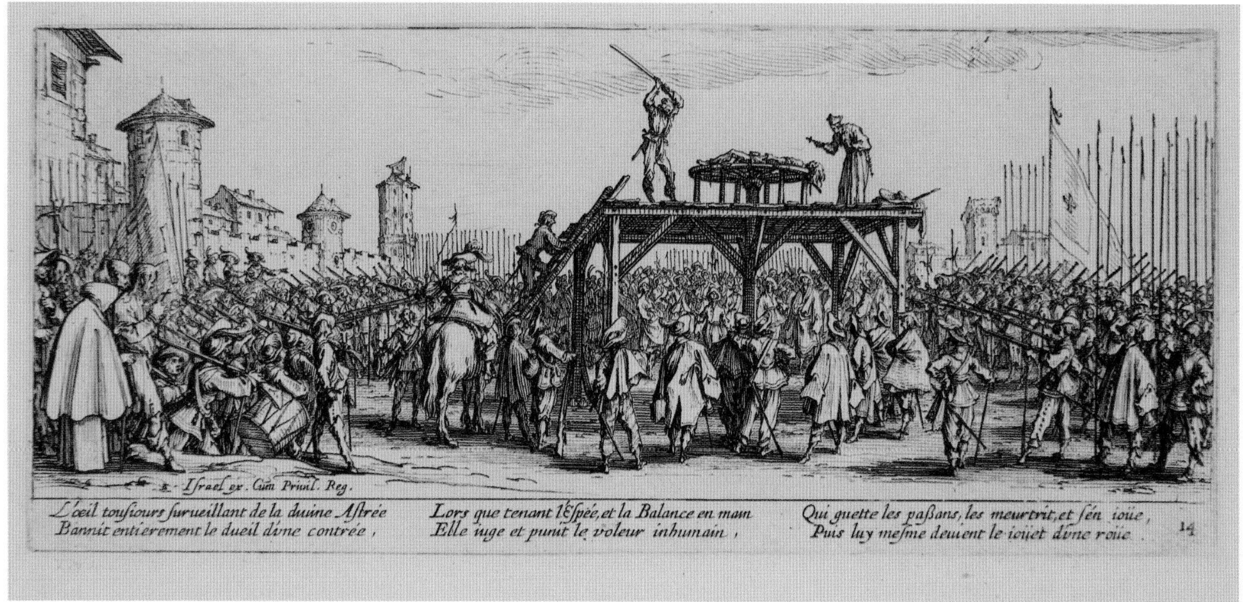

PLATE 15

The Hospital

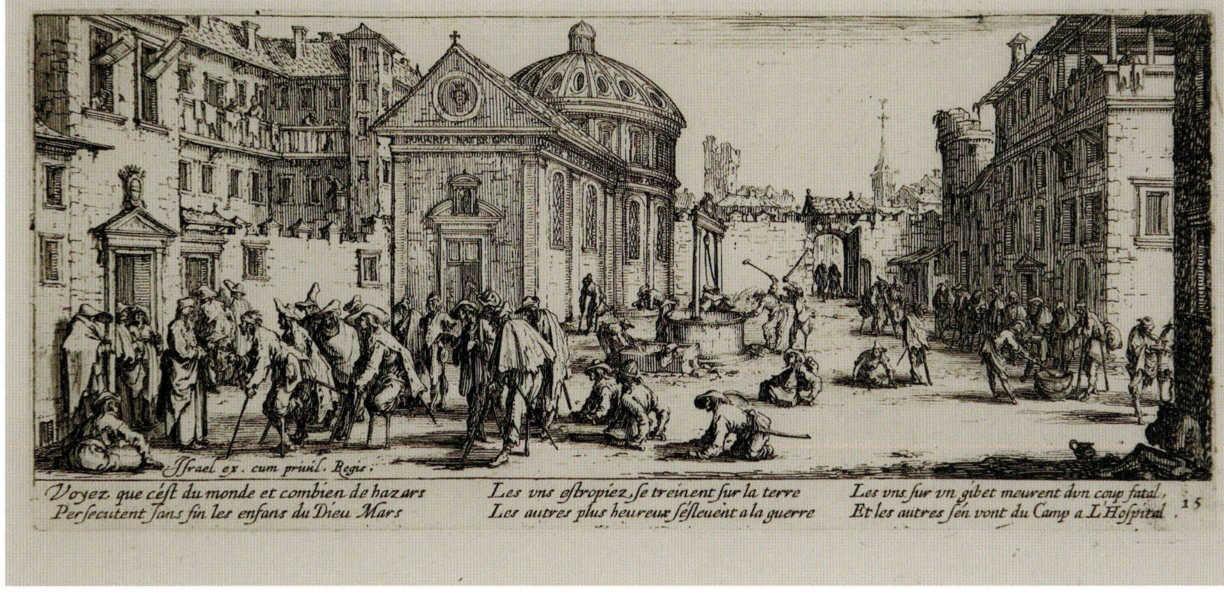

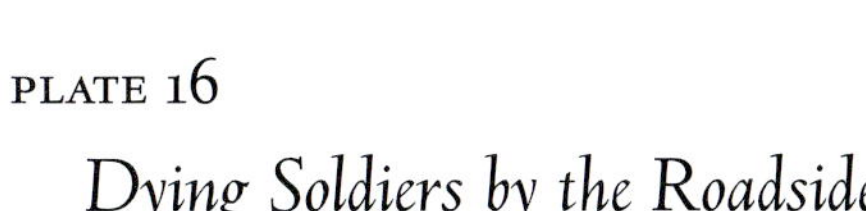

PLATE 16

Dying Soldiers by the Roadside

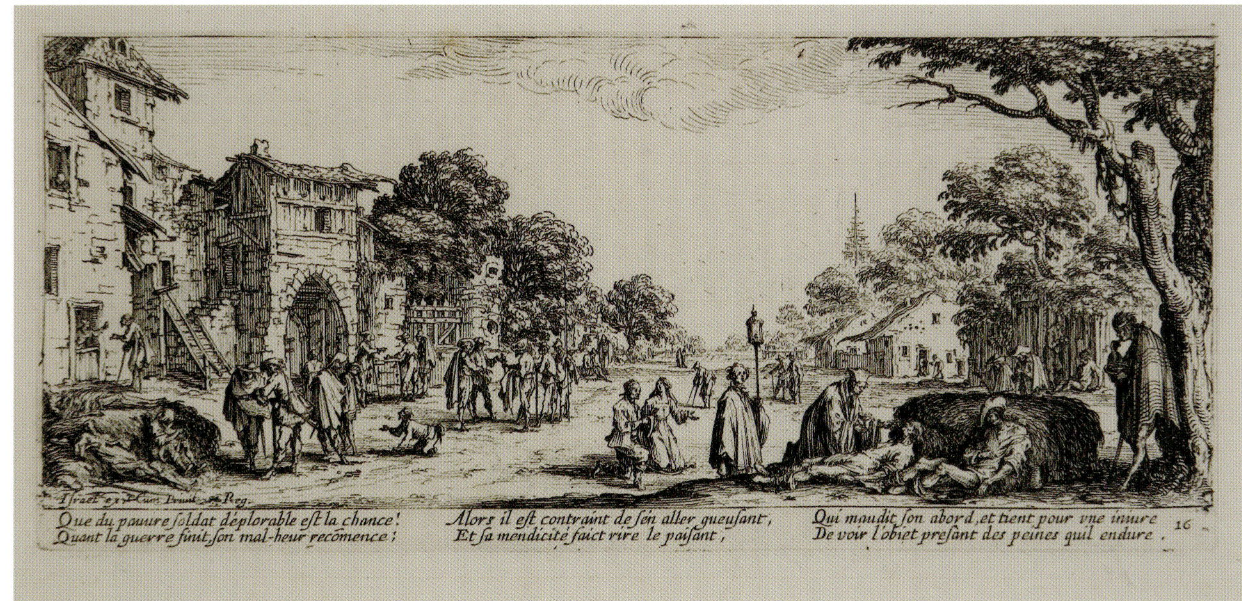

PLATE 17

Revenge of the Peasants

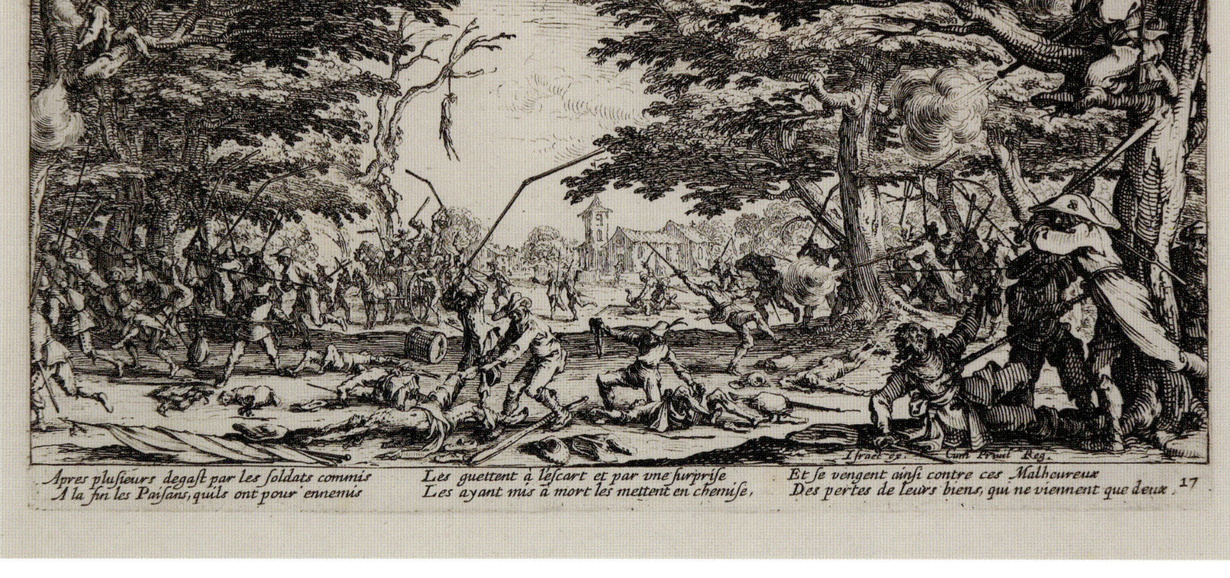

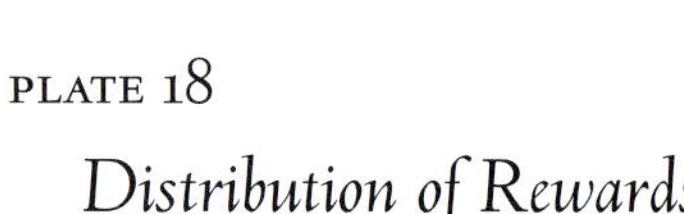

PLATE 18

Distribution of Rewards

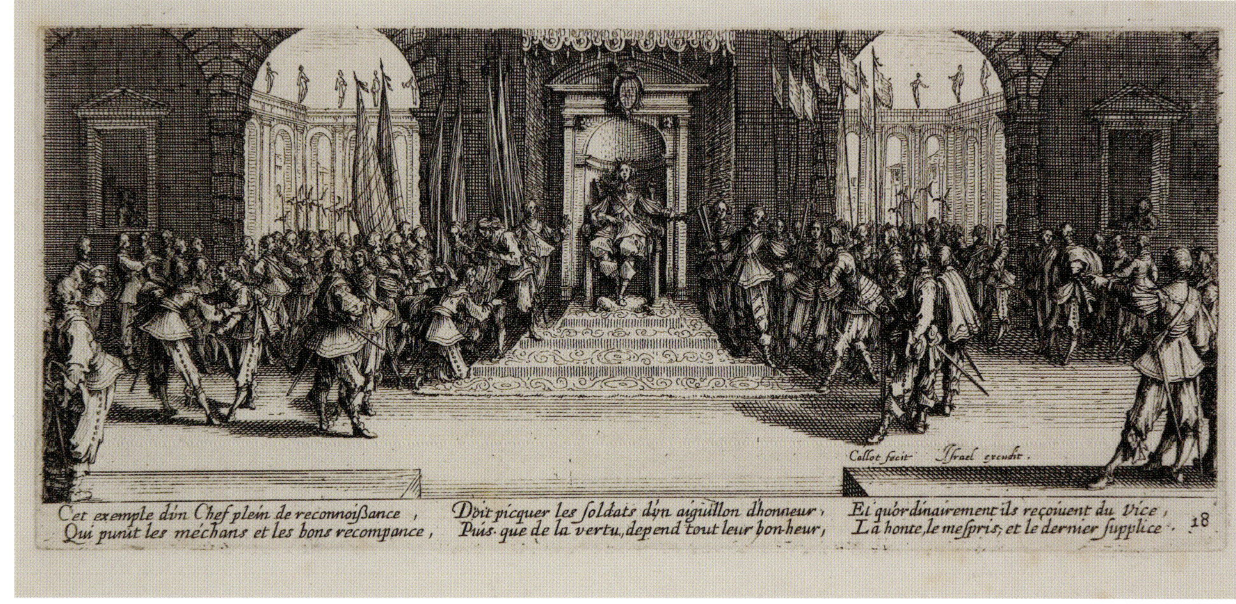

Sandow Birk at HuiPress

BY PAUL MULLOWNEY, ARTISTIC DIRECTOR, HUI NO'EAU VISUAL ARTS CENTER

SANDOW Birk's 2005 project in the print studio at Hui No'eau Visual Arts Center, a portfolio of etchings called *The Leading Causes of Death in America,* was one of the earliest and most important projects of the newly created HuiPress publishing enterprise. The project was inspired by the work of the early-twentieth-century American artist George Bellows and was commissioned by the San Diego Museum of Art for its *Contemporary Links* exhibition program.

As Director of the press, I had begun, in 2004, a printmaking residency program, inviting established and emerging artists to come to work in our studios, with the idea that given freedom and time to work, in a setting which is quiet and secluded, artists would create their best work. I had been going at it about a year when I was fortunate enough to be introduced to Sandow by my friend Catharine Clark, who represents Sandow in San Francisco.

For the *Death in America* series, we worked for two weeks in the studio in the medium of direct gravure, an etching process, similar to photogravure, that dates back to the nineteenth century. The process achieved the deep black tonal ranges for which Bellows' lithographs were known and allowed Sandow the freedom to make corrections directly on the copper plates (figs. 7). Each morning Sandow was out early surfing Ho'okipa, the famed north-shore spot on Maui, while my assistants and I worked on etching the gravure plates. In the afternoon we were proofing, Sandow making plate corrections, then starting the next drawings, working late into the night in our artists' cottage. He took to new materials quickly, with ease and intelligence – always a sign of talent in an artist who is approaching a new medium in printmaking. I was taken by his easygoing attitude, yet his discipline and his approach to his work had a perfect balance of humor and seriousness. He worked on the series quickly and decisively, and over two more proofing sessions the eleven prints which comprise *The Leading Causes of Death in America* turned out to be not only a beautiful and skilled tribute to Bellows, but also a sharp criticism of the American way of life, which seems to be killing us faster than we realize.

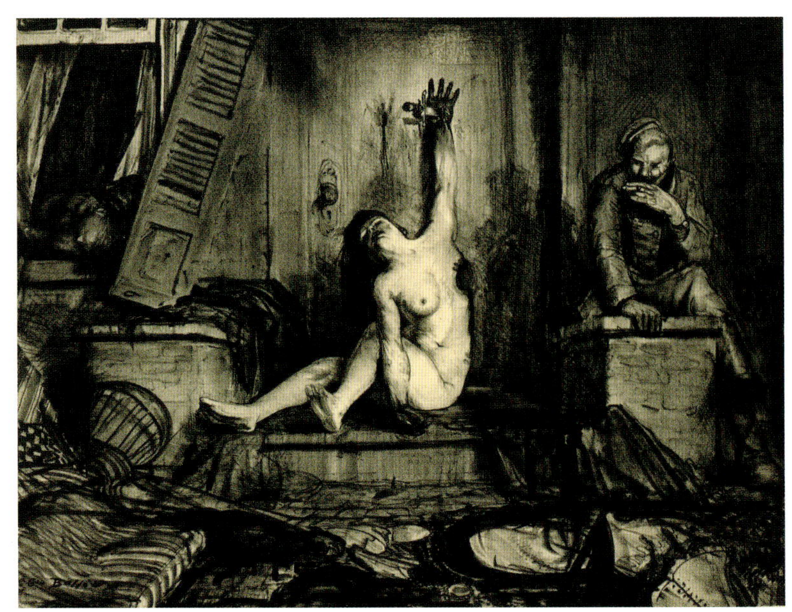

FIG. 6 George Bellows, *The Cigarette*

In sheer size and scope, *The Depravities of War* was a radical departure for Birk and the studio as a whole. It was a project that lasted more than a year and involved Sandow making several trips back and forth between Los Angeles and Maui. Teams of assistants – including Rhode Island School of Design interns Samuel Carr-Prindle and Nichol Markowitz working beside Elyse Pignolet, Sandow, and assistants Casey Neumann and Katherine Godwin – spent long hours routing, grinding and gouging the images in 4-by-8-foot birch plywood. It was a crazy scene of sometimes four people on a block at once (they finished the very last block, *Execution*, in just two days), the young printers with iPod earphones plugged in under ear-protection muffs for six hours straight, a mound of burnt carving bits on the floor, until our neighbor who lives across the banana tree break out back finally stopped me in a restaurant one night to complain of the constant noise. We had paper sent in specially from Japan, thin and handmade, because we have no press large enough to print thick sheets of western paper. Thin Japanese sheets large enough are rare and prohibitively expensive, so we seamed together sheets of *sekishu kozo* paper. Then we printed the blocks, backed the sheets for strength and stability, backed them again, and dried them flat by pasting them to large shellac-coated boards made for the project. The entire undertaking was led by the careful diligence of HuiPress head printer, Casey Neumann, to whom I am very grateful.

We owe much to these hard-working printers, yet they are historically anonymous craftsmen behind the scenes. Kathan Brown, the founder of San Francisco's esteemed Crown Point Press, and my life mentor in all things relating to printmaking, once remarked to me that history isn't kind to printers – their names are more often than not forgotten, as the artists, and to some extent the publishers themselves, receive all the credit. This is perhaps as it should be, and if it is true that printers are forgotten, still, as a group we are very grateful to Sandow Birk who is always patient and optimistic in his approach to this collaborative effort. We look forward to many more projects in the future as HuiPress grows and his work continues to be a vital contribution to the ongoing dialogue in American art.

It is with great pride that HuiPress Publications presents this extraordinary body of prints to the world through this catalog and the touring exhibition in the coming two years. I am grateful to Hui No'eau's new executive director, Deb Michaels, who supported the project and the catalog from the beginning of her tenure, and to the entire Board of Trustees at the Hui, who have had the wisdom to see that HuiPress publications remain funded and supported.

And I am indebted to the hard work and foresight of Greg Escalante and Andrea Harris-McGee at Grand Central Art Center, who have made sure that the reach of the project is as broad as it can be.

The ambitious *Depravities of War* project is a major milestone for this young print studio, but I also believe at this juncture in history it will be a very important contribution to American contemporary printmaking as a whole. With this epic body of work, Sandow Birk certainly places himself firmly in the long tradition of graphic journalistic war reporting that traces directly back to the prints of Jacques Callot and Francisco Goya and to the work of countless other artists throughout the centuries who were brave enough and keen enough to record the horrors of war through the medium of printmaking. It is my belief that, at the end of the day in American art, this body of work will be as enduring as the work of George Bellows himself, who inspired Birk's earlier project at HuiPress and whose prints also addressed the eternal subject of the horrors of war and the injustices and torpor of modern society.

As Catharine Clark asks in her catalog essay – what is next? Unfortunately for humanity, the calamities continue unabated; but fortunately for us, there will always be artists such as Sandow Birk who will continue to riff on the foibles of mankind by holding up the mirror into which we must gaze.

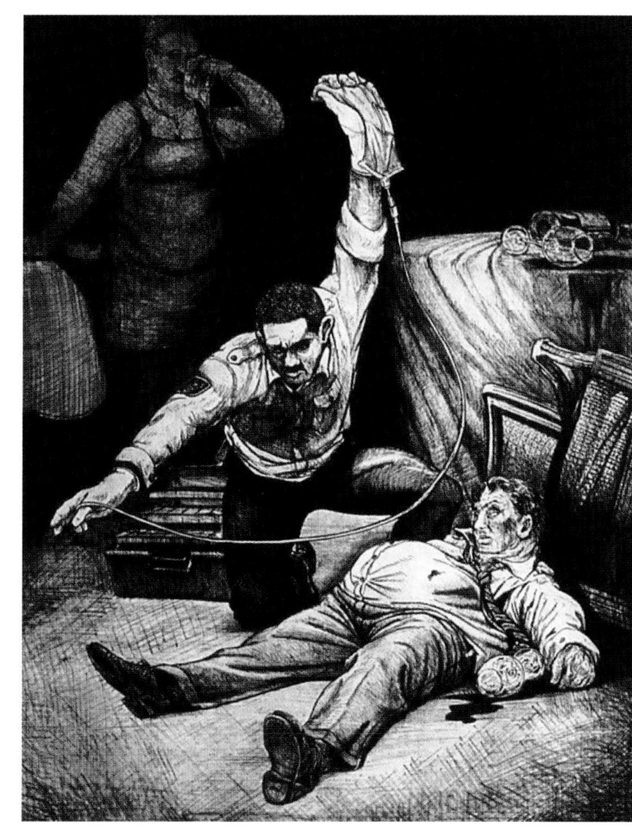

FIG. 7 Sandow Birk, *Heart Attack*

As the last chapter in the present conflict in Iraq hopefully comes to a speedy cessation; as the horrific images of events there begin to fade from our collective memory – the velocity of collective memory loss now being as catastrophic as wars themselves; and as the hanging of Saddam becomes a messy footnote in our history, perhaps – who knows? – the iconic images that emerge a hundred or even two hundred years from now in the collective consciousness won't be Internet video postings or newspaper photographs at all, but for a future generation they might well be these images by American artist Sandow Birk.

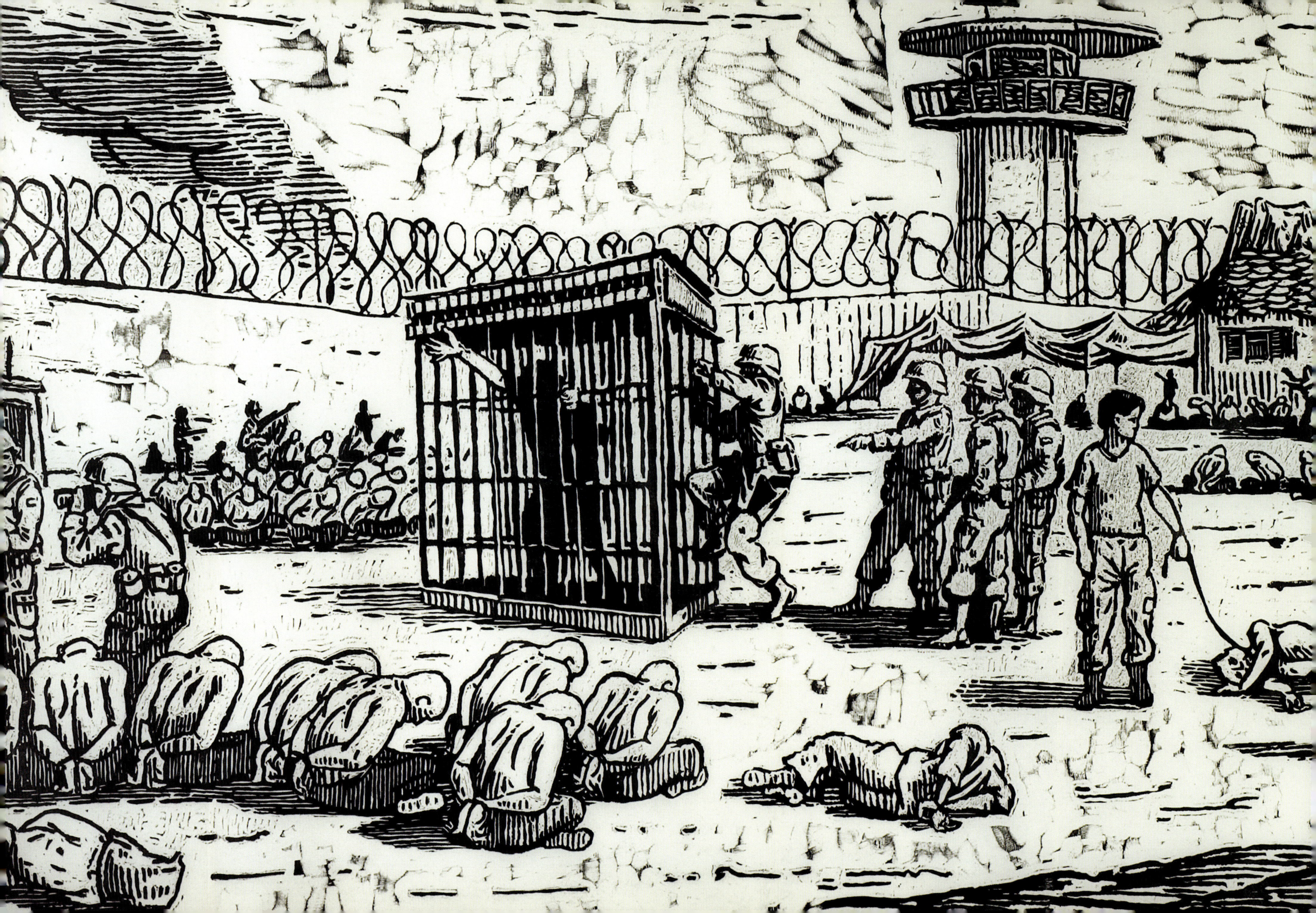

Printmaking in Protest

BY MARILYN VIERRA, DIRECTOR OF PROGRAMS AND EXHIBITIONS, HUI NOʻEAU VISUAL ARTS CENTER

SANDOW Birk's *The Depravities of War* series fits into the continuum, beginning in the seventeenth century, in which artists have used printmaking media to convey of the human capacity for inhumanity during wartime. The works of Jacques Callot (1592-1635) and Francisco de Goya (1746-1828), with Honoré Daumier (1798-1879), Pablo Picasso (1891-1973), and James Rosenquist (b. 1933) following suit, form much of the legacy of this genre of printmaking. The appeal of printmaking media to artists motivated by the horrors and injustice of war resides in the replicable nature of prints and thus their ability to carry information to an audience broader than that which a single painting can reach.

Birk's *Depravities* are 4-by-8-foot woodblock prints made on sheets of Japanese paper; they are neither easily disseminated nor widely replicable in their original form. This inversion, as it were, of the cultural purpose of printmaking is hardly accidental. Birk mines the most accessible communication media in history – cable-television news productions and the Internet – for his images, and he mimics our collective predilection for cinematic news coverage with the scale of his prints. By employing the oldest printmaking medium on a grand scale, he offers anachronistically traditional renditions of his high tech-generated source material. Indeed, because Birk invents no new imagery, but combines passages from hundreds of different news-media still photographs with the compositional conventions of academic history painting, he actually comments on the way in which we are informed. He presents this commentary as boldly in the paradox of his cool, banal style and the roughness of the medium as he does in the visual content itself.[1]

The immediacy of "embedded" reporting formulated in the early months of the Iraq war is paralleled by Birk's working methods – the fifteen large plywood sheets he used were laid out and carved rapidly, sometimes within days (*Execution*, plate 32) of the events they depict. The prints testify to this haste, as the roughness of line and grain of the panels are clearly discernable. Technical process is articulated unedited in the same intentional manner as is our "news" from the front.

How does the instantaneous nature of visual evidence of news events affect our interpretation of these events? We know that the power of images delivered with the preamble "breaking news" can render vast fallacy indelible on popular memory. This is the context of Sandow Birk's source imagery. In Paul Virilio's recent work, *The Information Bomb* (2000), the French philosopher and cultural theorist expresses his ideas about the ways in which the almost-instantaneous transmission of information and imagery through today's media mimics the effects of socioeconomic and political globalization.[2] Empirical scientific method, he posits, is being replaced by "extreme science…moving away from patient research into reality to become part of a generalized virtualization."[3] He continues "…this techno-science becomes, then, as mass techno-culture, the agent not, as in the past, of the acceleration of history, but of the dizzying whirl of the acceleration of reality – and that to the detriment of all verisimilitude."[4] Applying these ideas to journalism renders rationality of reportage rather secondary. Similarly, in cases where remote events are reported, we have the images first, creating the illusion of nearness. Whether from the camera of an embedded reporter, a cell-phone camera of a soldier, or a podcast, the all-day news junkie can fancy him- or herself in possession of ample material from which to derive accurate and relevant conclusions. We know from the ultimate "truth" of the Jessica Lynch rescue, for example, that there is always room and, evidently, reason for fictional "spin."

Returning to the antiwar canon, it is useful to compare the printmaking media, source imagery, and the expressive intentions of Callot, Goya and Daumier with those of Birk, who channels elements of his predecessors' media and messages into his own sub-genre based on appropriation of formal elements and concepts. Callot, in his series of etchings titled *The Miseries of War* (1630s, plates 1–18), which Birk studied for his *Depravities* project, appears oriented to reportage, providing minute detail in his observation of the execution of war. Goya's depictions of war subjects are haunting interpretations not just of depraved acts, but also of their consequences to humanity. Daumier's prints, among the first to truly reach the masses, began the history of artists collaborating with writers to comment in print on the plight of the common person.

Callot was not trained as a painter but received early training as a goldsmith in his native Nancy, in the region of Lorraine, and continued with studies in engraving in Rome and Florence from 1608-21. During his early years in Italy, he adapted his technique to etching. Callot's etchings from his years in the court of Cosimo de Medici, as well as his *Miseries of War* series, bear the stamp of traditional history painting in their expansive, fully schematized perspective and formulaic compositions. He depicted the lavish festivals of the Florentine court in tremendous detail, seeming to delight in the outlandish costumes and imaginative dramatizations of these themed events.[5] Callot was a great technical innovator, developing an etching stylus, the *échoppe*, which could render fluid, elegant lines similar to those achieved in engraving while exploiting the more flexible, expressive qualities of etching. He also introduced a ground more durable than the waxed grounds in use at the time, allowing etched results that were considerably more predictable.[6]

Callot returned to his native Lorraine in the 1620s as the Thirty Years' War raged. He observed first hand the events of the war and in the 1630s began the first series of prints in the antiwar canon, *The Miseries of War*, in which he represented the plight of the peasants and soldiers amidst warring monarchies (plates 1–18). Like Callot's images, Birk's action tableaux express a chronological aspect of a specific war. Although *The Depravities of War* may be Birk's commentary upon the current war in Iraq and the way in which it is portrayed in contemporary news-media, his printmaking vocabulary and grammar are quite familiar. Each of the prints is orchestrated with attention to "correct" perspective and pictorial conventions, such as *repoussé* elements in shadow at the foreground edges, balanced diagonals in the action of the scene, and clear progression of spatial planes from foreground to distance. Birk seems to offer a primer of such conventions in the totality of this series, augmenting and even informing his commentary by the formal aspects of his art making. Perhaps his predilection for these historicizing compositional conventions drew him to Callot's series of seventeen etchings. Birk's borrowings from Callot are clear and take different forms. In general, Birk and Callot emphasize the impact of war on the everyday lives and settings of indigenous populations, forming stark contrasts between architecture and people in established cultures and the mechanics of their destruction. Birk quotes compositional passages from Callot, as in replacing Callot's Roman temple of *The Hospital* (plate 15) with a mosque in his own *Destruction* (plate 24). In *Repercussion* (plate 33), Birk mines the same Callot composition for architectural elements and figure groupings as well as spatial organization. *The Hanging Tree* by Callot (plate 11) brings to mind the topic of Birk's much differently composed *Execution*. Themes of cruelty and humiliation run commonly throughout the work of each artist, with Birk's images relating to the Abu Ghraib prison scandal in *Degradation* (plate 29) and *Humiliation* (plate 30) the most provocative, challenging prints in his series.

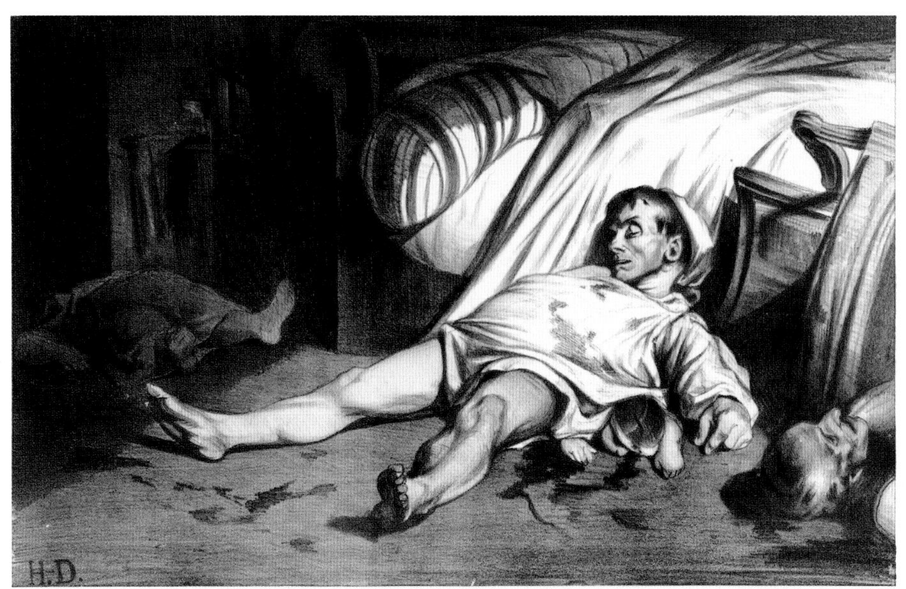

FIG. 8 Honoré Daumier, *Rue Transnonian*

Birk further aligns with Callot by offering very little philosophizing within his imagery. His simple, one-word titles, similar in their brevity to Callot's, allude proverbially to lessons in progress without referring literally to the war in Iraq. There is no caricaturing in this work; its power comes from a lexicon of visual referents furnished relentlessly and often without context by every visual aspect of our global media. The atrocities depicted by Birk are not the gruesome details of the battlefield but instead are identified in the humiliation of Iraqis by U.S. troops. At an extreme point of interpretation, his figures often recall the tiny plastic toy soldiers sold by the bucket at toy stores.

Whereas Callot and Goya drew on first-hand experiences of wars in places familiar to them, Birk activates his viewers' collective memory with scenes familiar through the news media. His experience is more removed from the actual events and places that he depicts, although if one adheres to the idea that he is depicting the nature of information transfer, one can say that his work is quite primary in nature.

Goya worked primarily in aquatint in the *Los Caprichos* (1796-98) series, producing moody, expressive results. For the *Desastres de la Guerra* etchings (c. 1820), Goya used old plates out of necessity driven by the wars with Napoleon, whose atrocities he depicts – metal was in short supply. The prints bear evidence of this recycling in their tattered lines and rough textures, which heighten the potency of the charged imagery.[7] Similarly, Birk chose woodcut for its technical immediacy and the possibility of carving fifteen of these very large scenes in a short period of time. Like Goya, Birk is primarily a painter who frequently produces prints in relation to his paintings.

Daumier worked in lithography in the mid-nineteenth century, when the emergent voice of the proletariat was reaching a fever pitch. He began publishing his prints, with written commentary by Charles Philipon, in a weekly paper devoted to political and social satire. Daumier's prolific output of provocative imagery is linked directly to the broad distribution of *La Caricature* and, after official censorship ended the publication of that weekly, *Le Charivari*, a much smaller weekly specializing in social rather than political satire.[8] The wide distribution of printed media introduced the Modern era, whose epilogue we are now living and of which Birk's *Depravities* series is certainly a part. Daumier's contribution of bold, expressive dramatizations of actual events (*Rue Transnonian*, 1834, fig. 8) and vituperative allegorical satire (*Gargantua*, 1831) depart significantly from the docudrama of Callot's prints. Although Birk works with materials available to us as part of the history of Daumier's image making, we recognize him as more closely aligned with Callot artistically and conceptually.[9] The tone of Birk's political commentary is less confrontational than that of Goya or Daumier because he renders an abundance of visual information in a curiously undercharged manner.

Birk's piecemeal quotations of news-media images in his *Depravities of War* series identify these prints as closer to themed chronology than to documentary. The artist maintains tension between the two by including two singularly themed prints – *Execution* (depicting the hanging of Saddam Hussein, plate 32), carved just days after the actual event in January 2007, and *Investigation* (depicting a Senate Hearing, plate 31). These prints seem intended to remind us that what we observe through the media is quite real at a fundamental level – and ultimately depraved in its entirety. He does not dwell on the details of the suffering, inhumanity, and immorality of the acts reassembled in his tableaux; he leaves the viewer to complete the new sentences he begins.

1 This cool banality aligns with the romanticism implicit in the genre of history painting. There, artists referenced ancient events and mythologies to allegorize fairly heinous contemporary realities, most often of war. In this series of prints, Birk plays conceptually upon the dichotomy between the harsh reality of photojournalistic imagery and its isolation from the human tragedy of war.

2 Paul Virilio, *The Information Bomb* (New York: Verso, 2000), 7-10.

3 Virilio, 2.

4 Virilio, 3.

5 Esther Averill, *Eyes on the World* (New York: Funk and Wagnalls, 1969), 16-49.

6 Donald Saff and Deli Sacilotto, *Printmaking: History and Process* (Thompson Learning, 1978), 98-99.

7 Saff and Sacilotto, *Printmaking: History and Process*, 108-110.

8 Saff and Sacilotto, *Printmaking: History and Process*, 188-91.

9 It is notable that Sandow Birk borrowed the composition of *Rue Transnonian* from Daumier in his *Heart Attack*, one of the etchings in his *Leading Causes of Death in America* series (2005)

SANDOW BIRK

The Depravities of War

SANDOW BIRK, *The Depravities of War*

Suite of fifteen woodcuts made in 2007, each 48 x 96 inches, on handmade *Sekishu* paper.

PLATE 19

Title Page

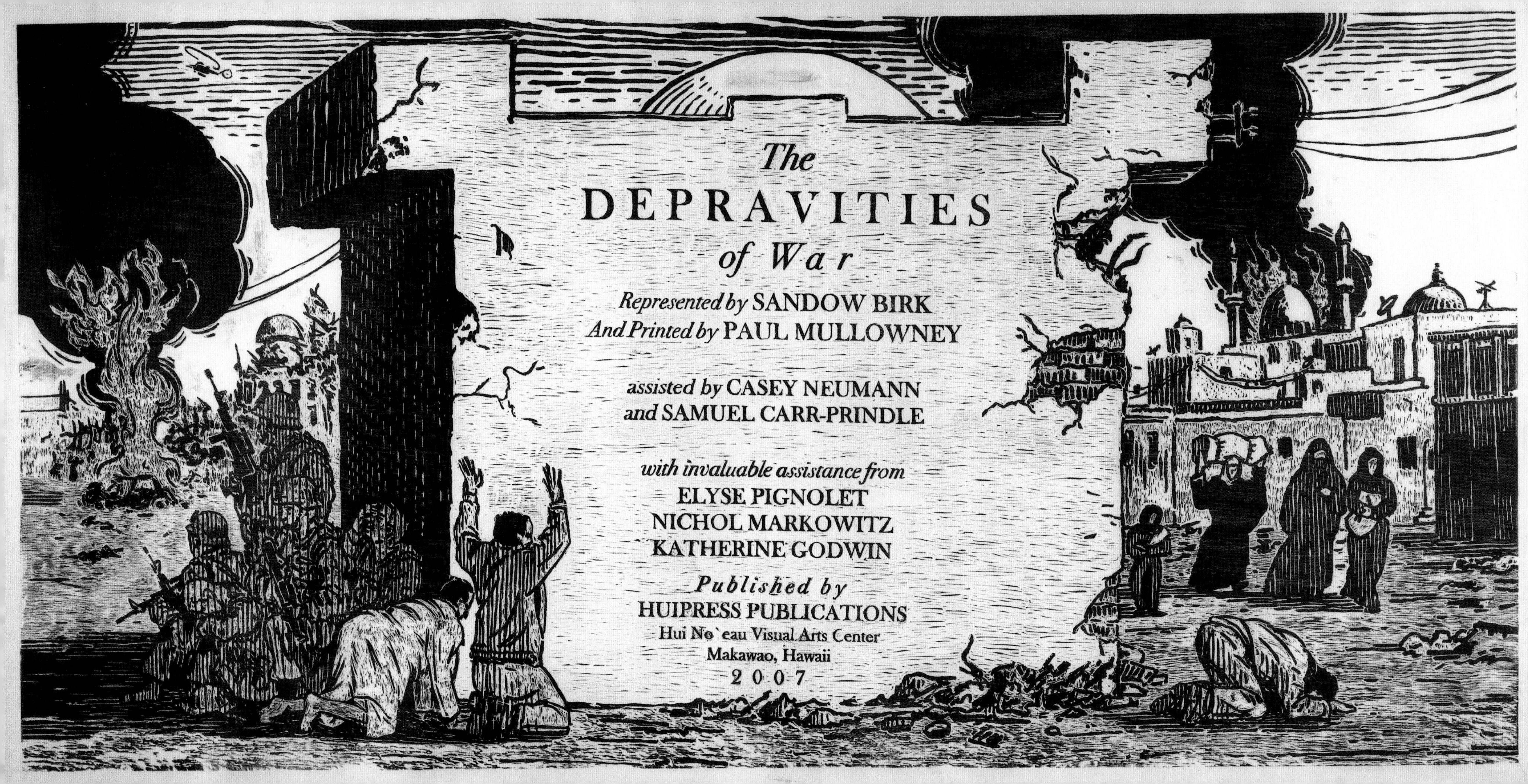
The
DEPRAVITIES
of War
Represented by SANDOW BIRK
And Printed by PAUL MULLOWNEY
assisted by CASEY NEUMANN
and SAMUEL CARR-PRINDLE
with invaluable assistance from
ELYSE PIGNOLET
NICHOL MARKOWITZ
KATHERINE GODWIN
Published by
HUIPRESS PUBLICATIONS
Hui No`eau Visual Arts Center
Makawao, Hawaii
2007

PLATE 20

Obsession

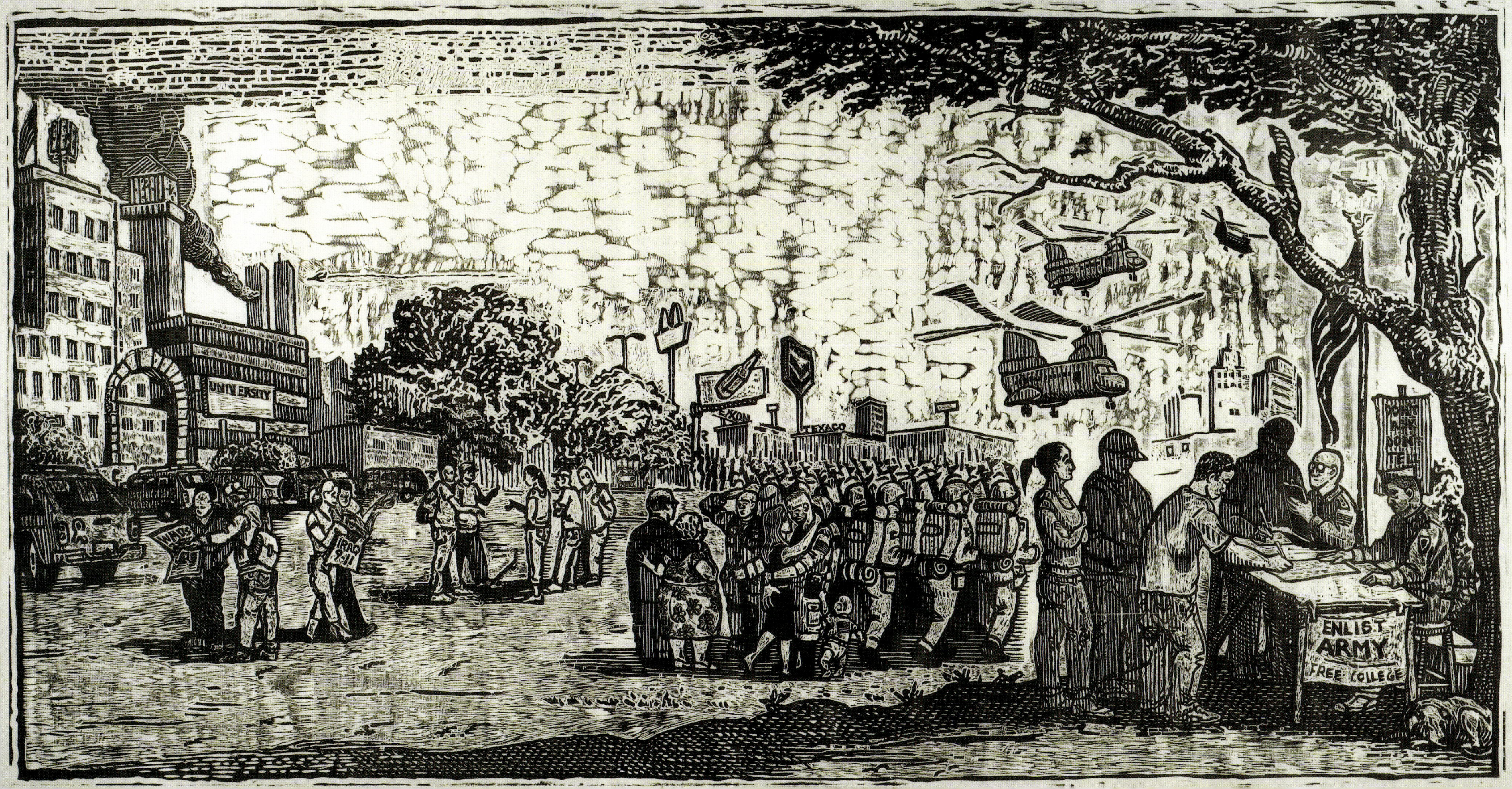
UNIVERSITY
IRAQ
9-11
TEXACO
ENLIST
ARMY
FREE COLLEGE

PLATE 21

Preparation

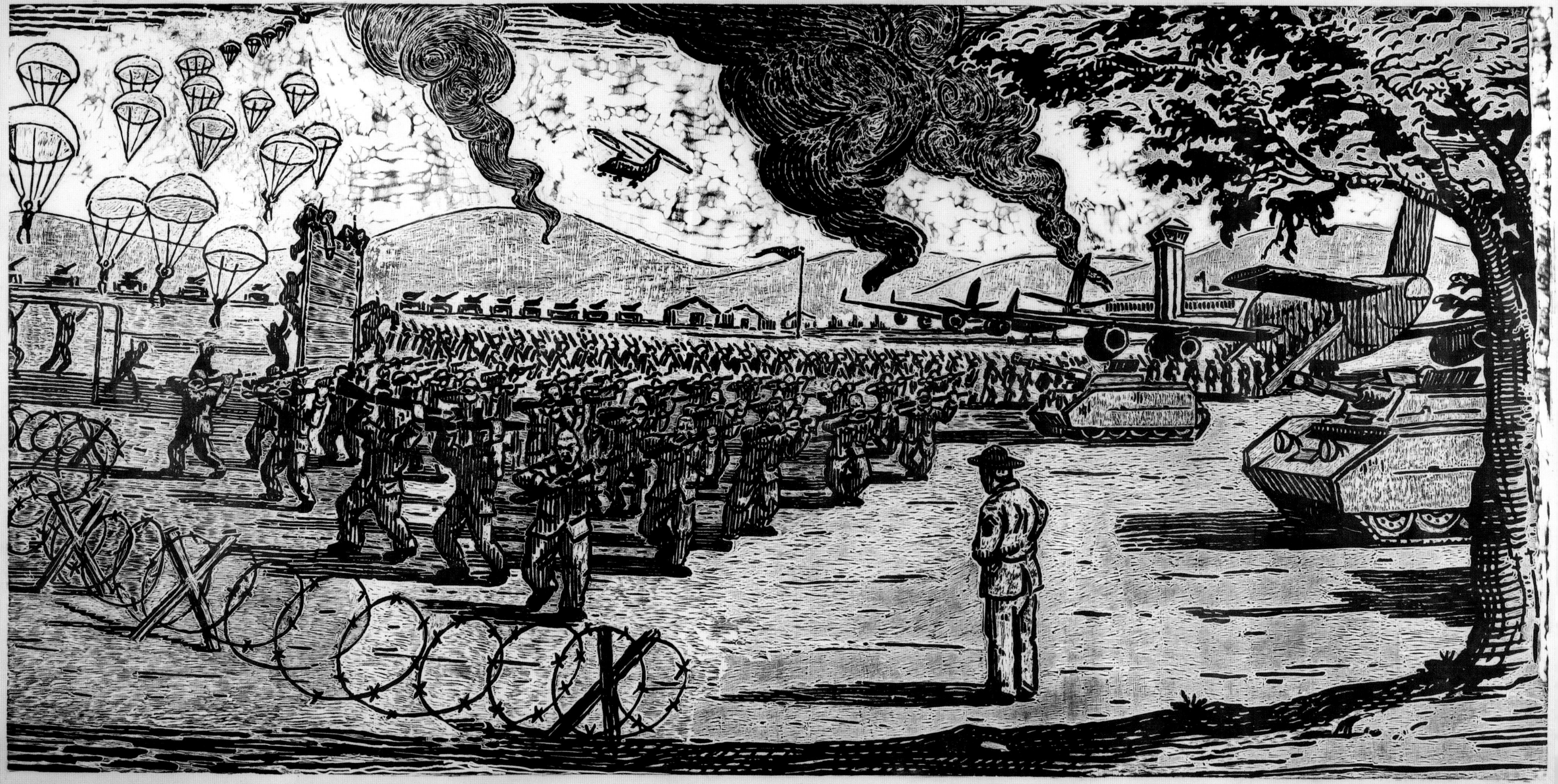

PLATE 22

Invasion

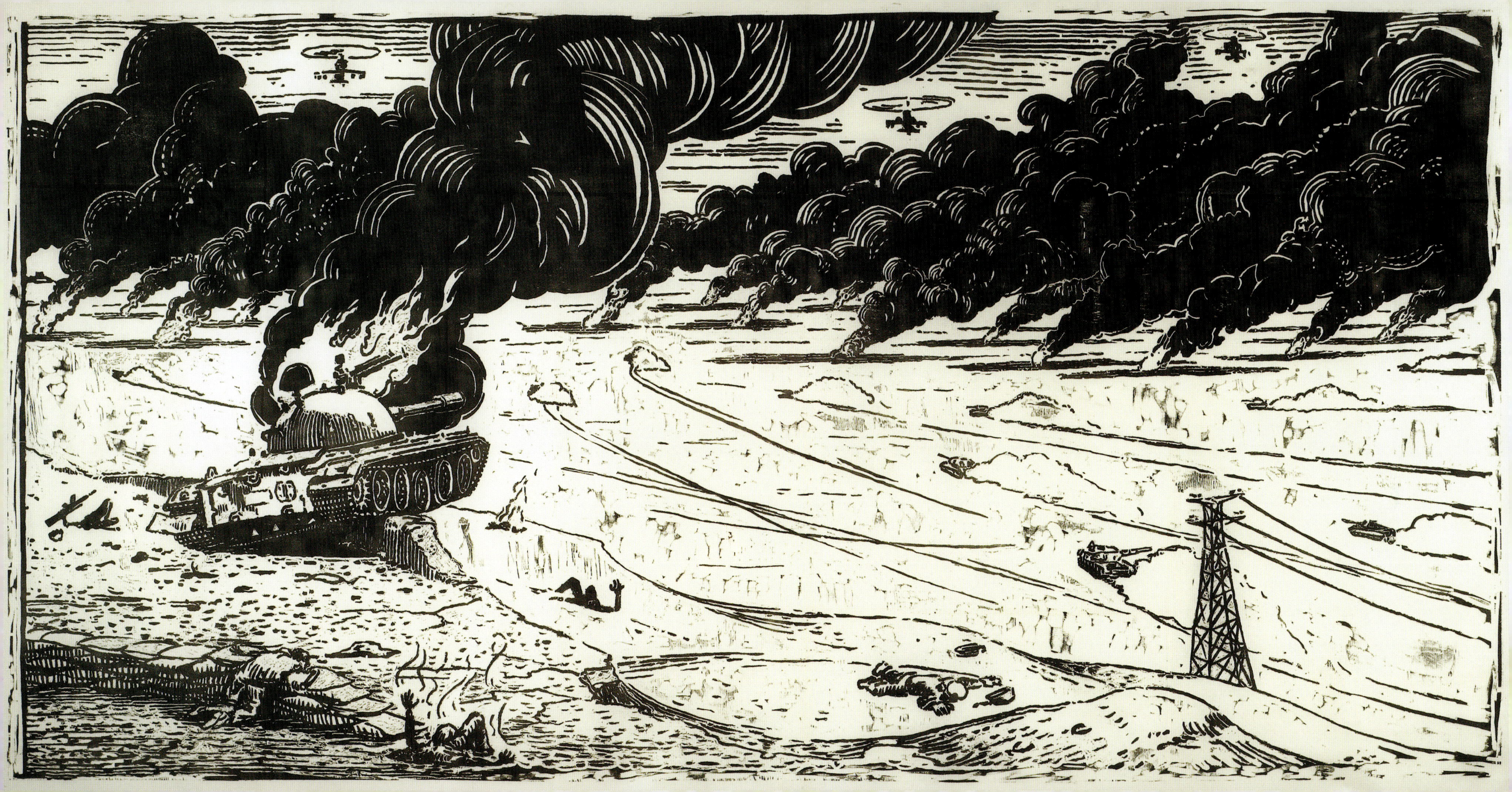

PLATE 23

Incursion

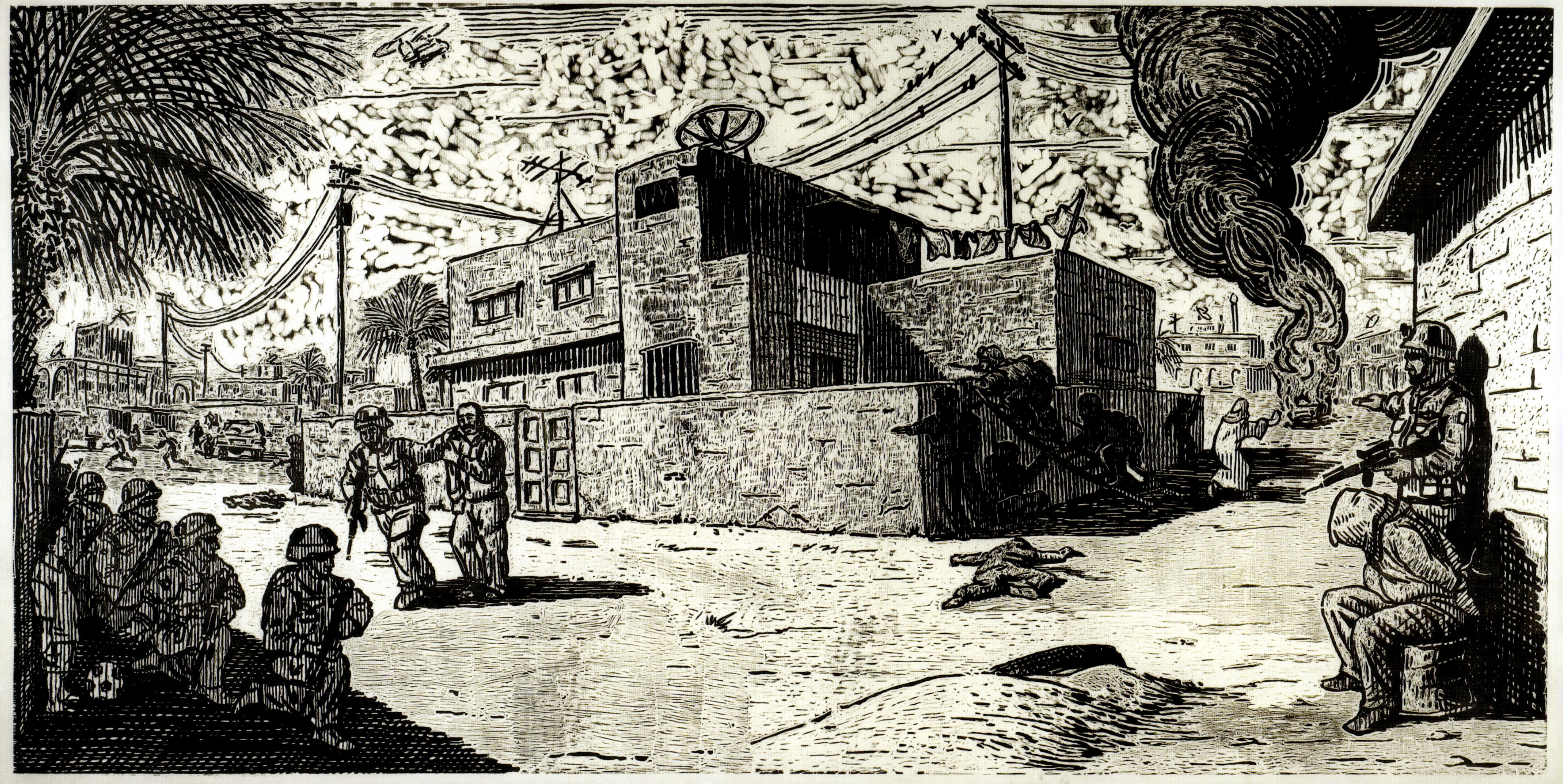

PLATE 24

Destruction

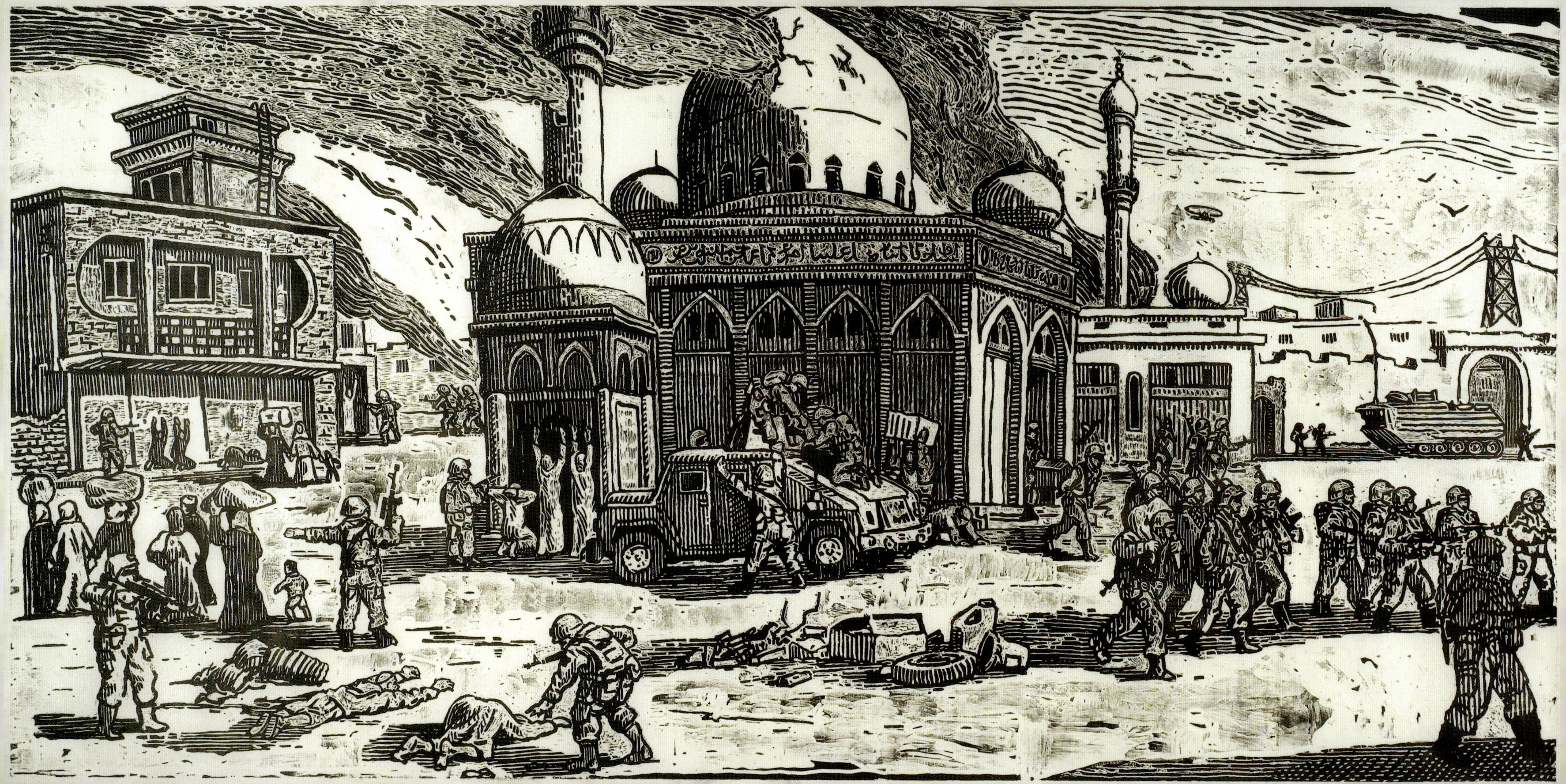

PLATE 25

Desecration

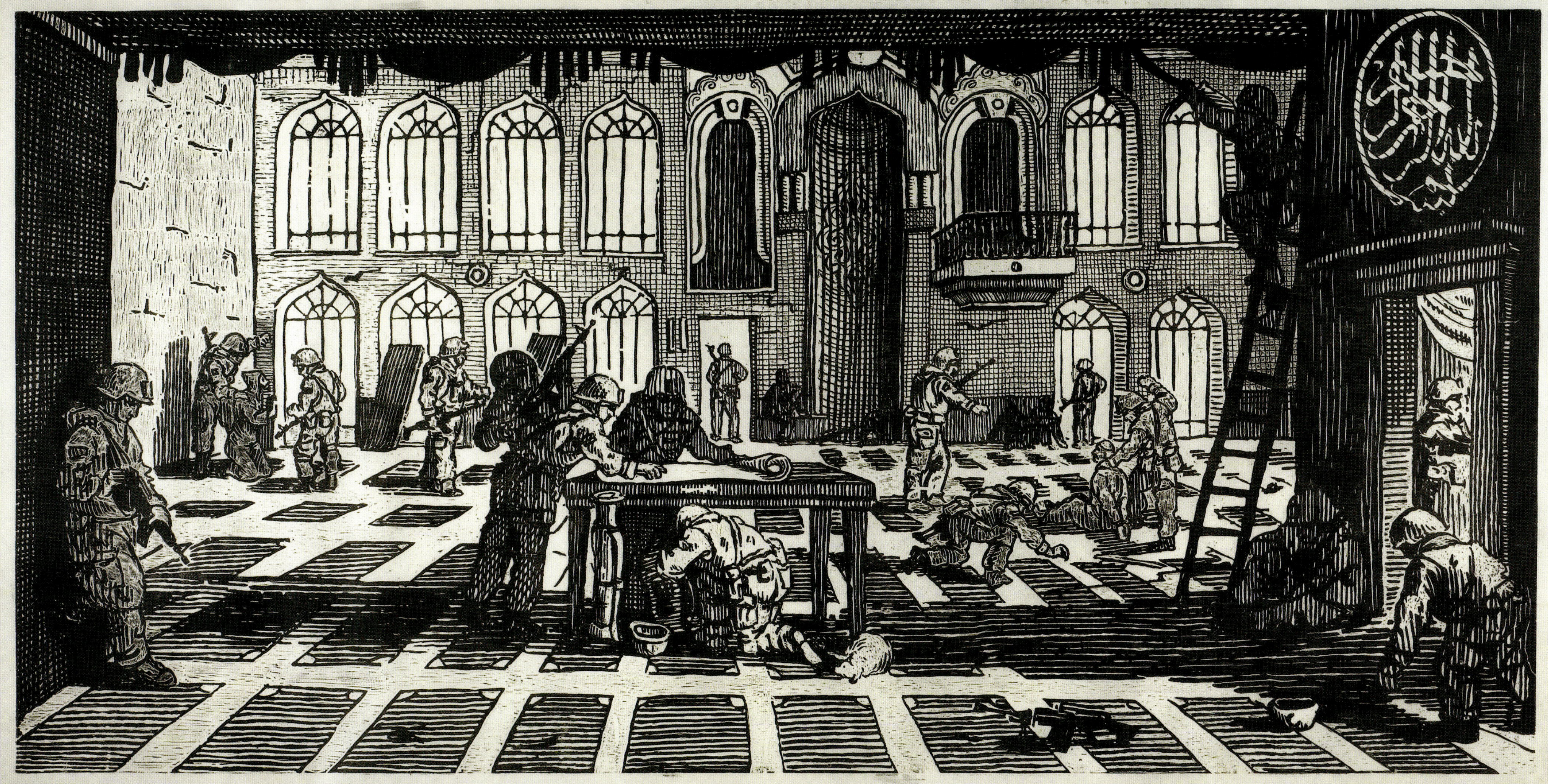

PLATE 26

Occupation

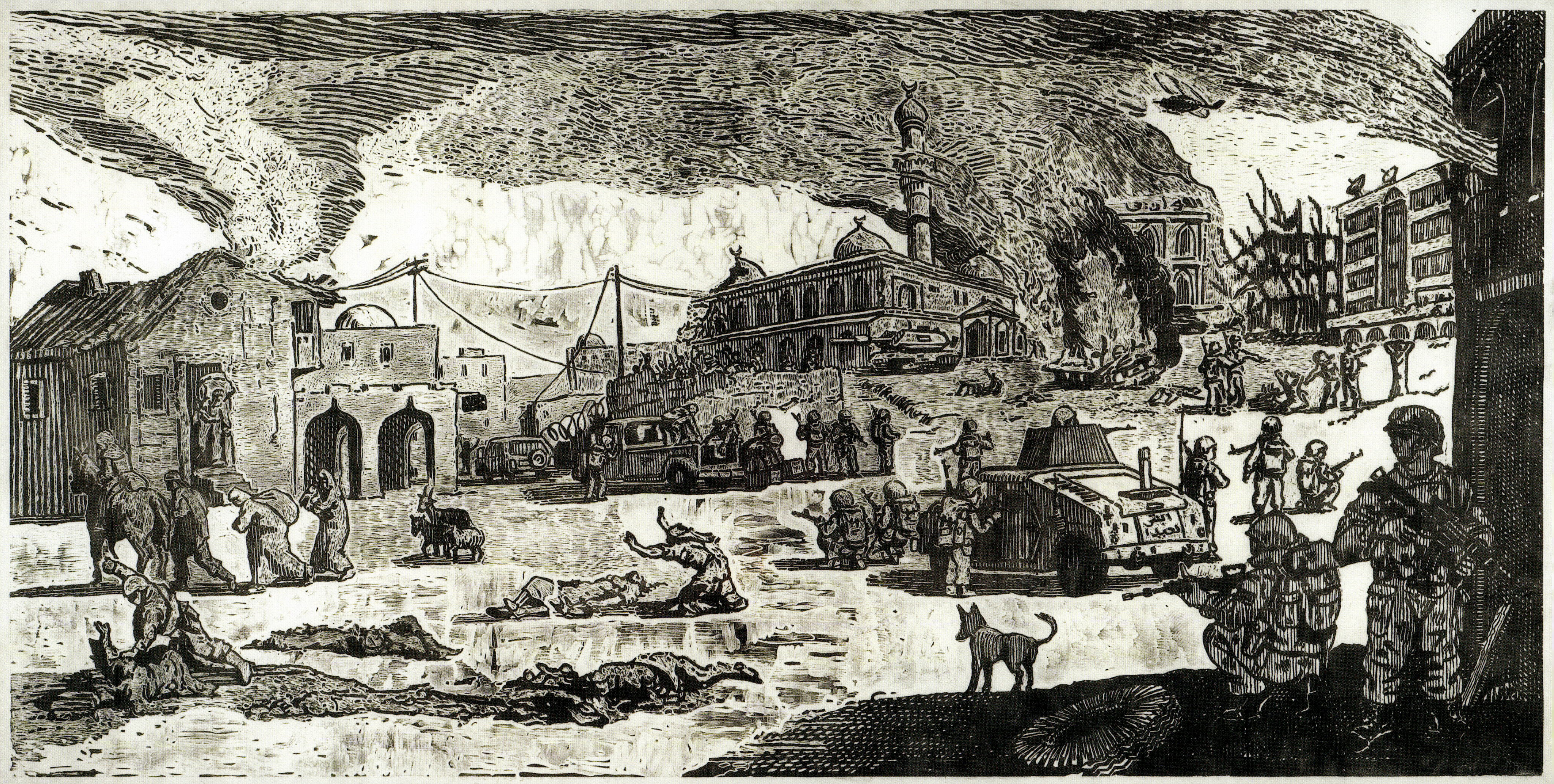

PLATE 27

Insurrection

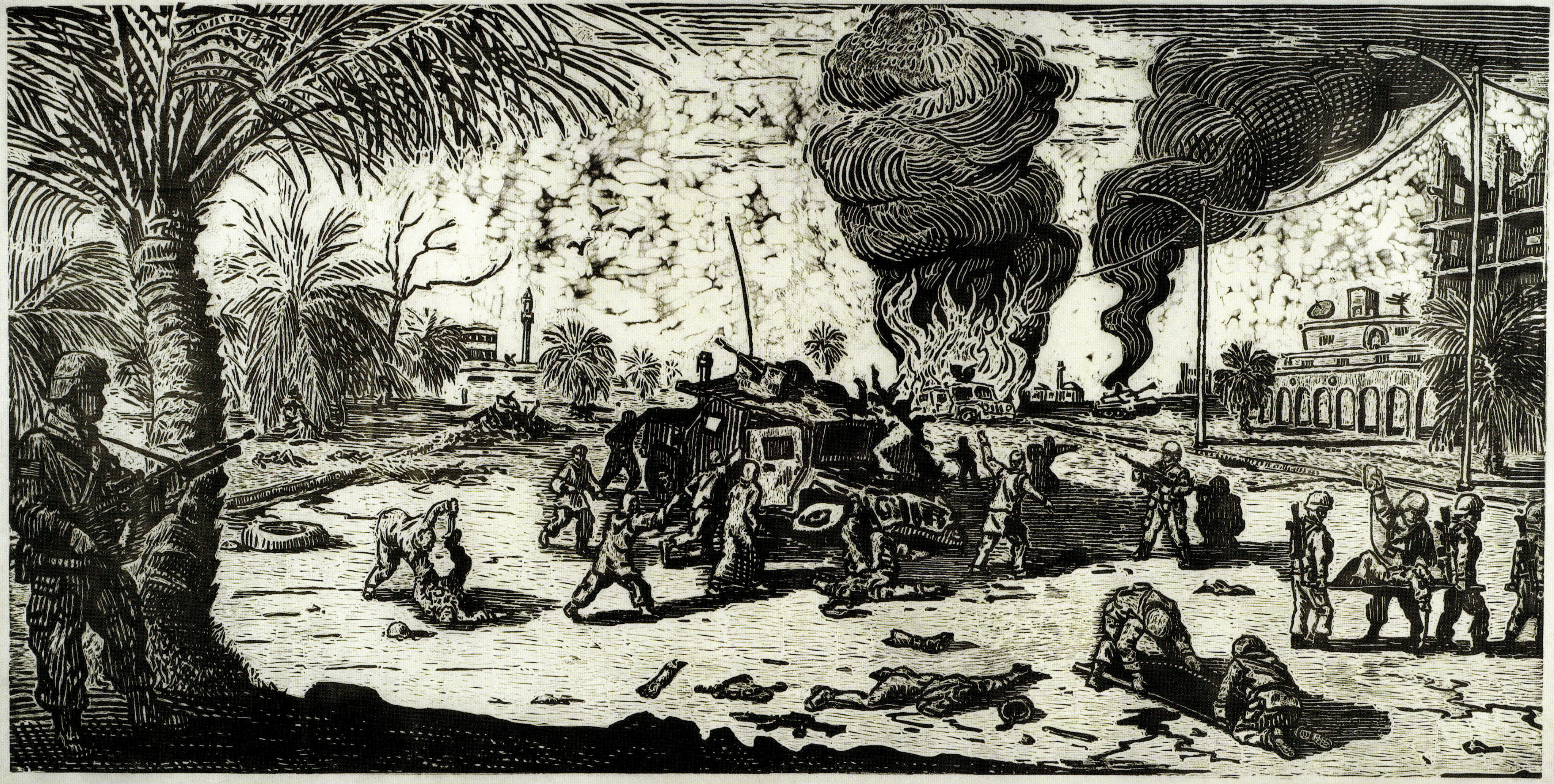

PLATE 28

Detention

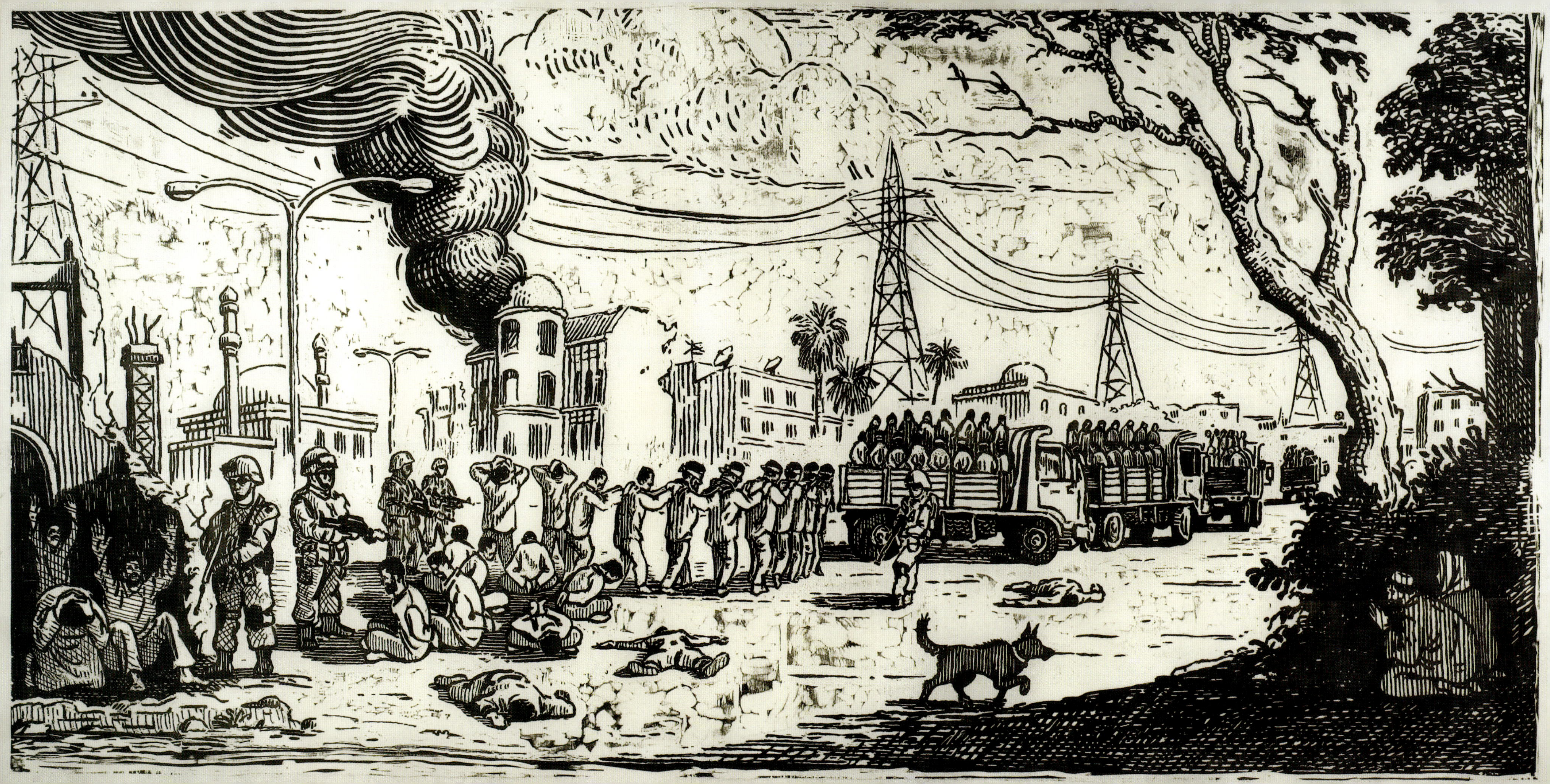

PLATE 29

Degradation

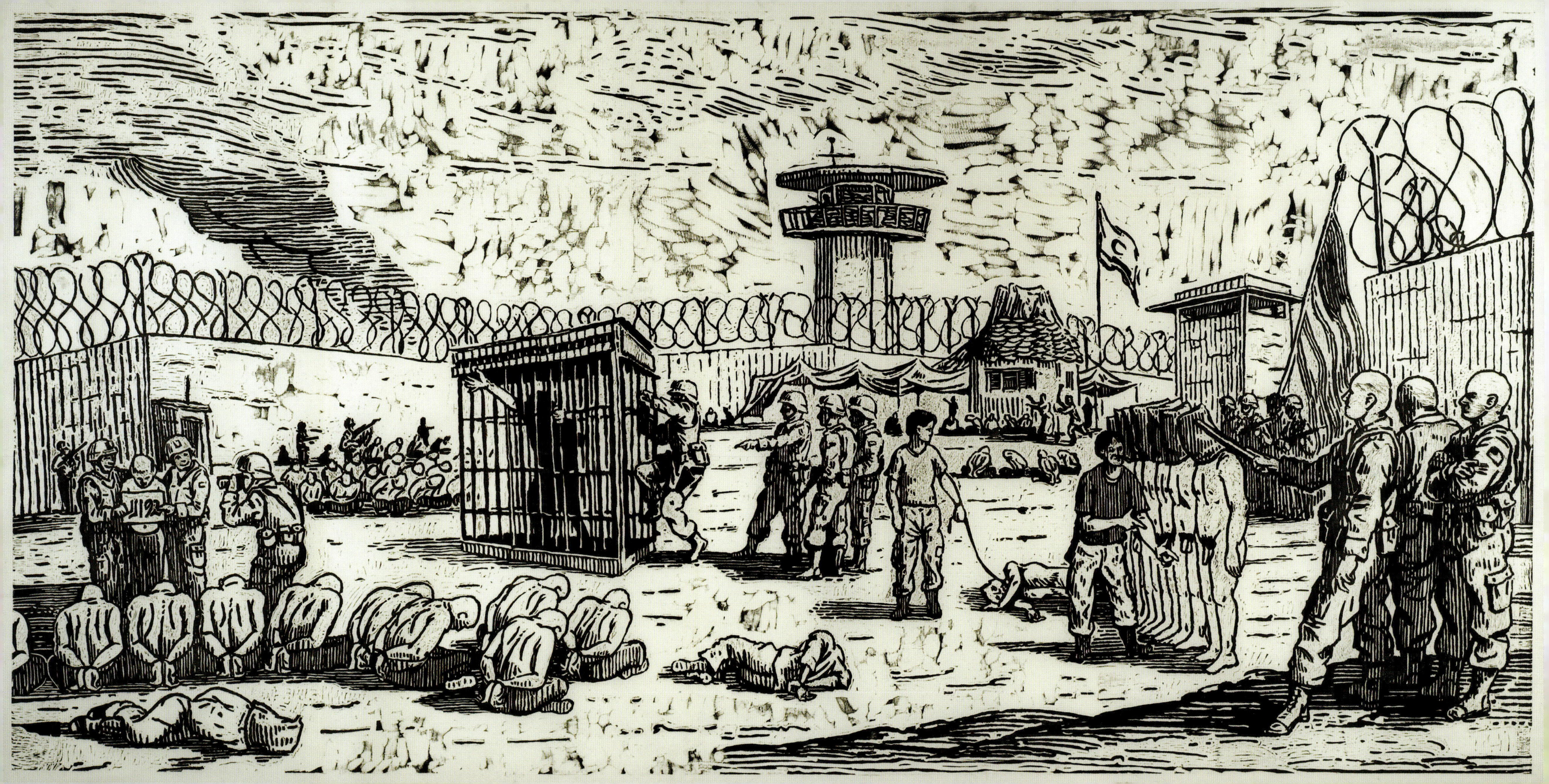

PLATE 30

Humiliation

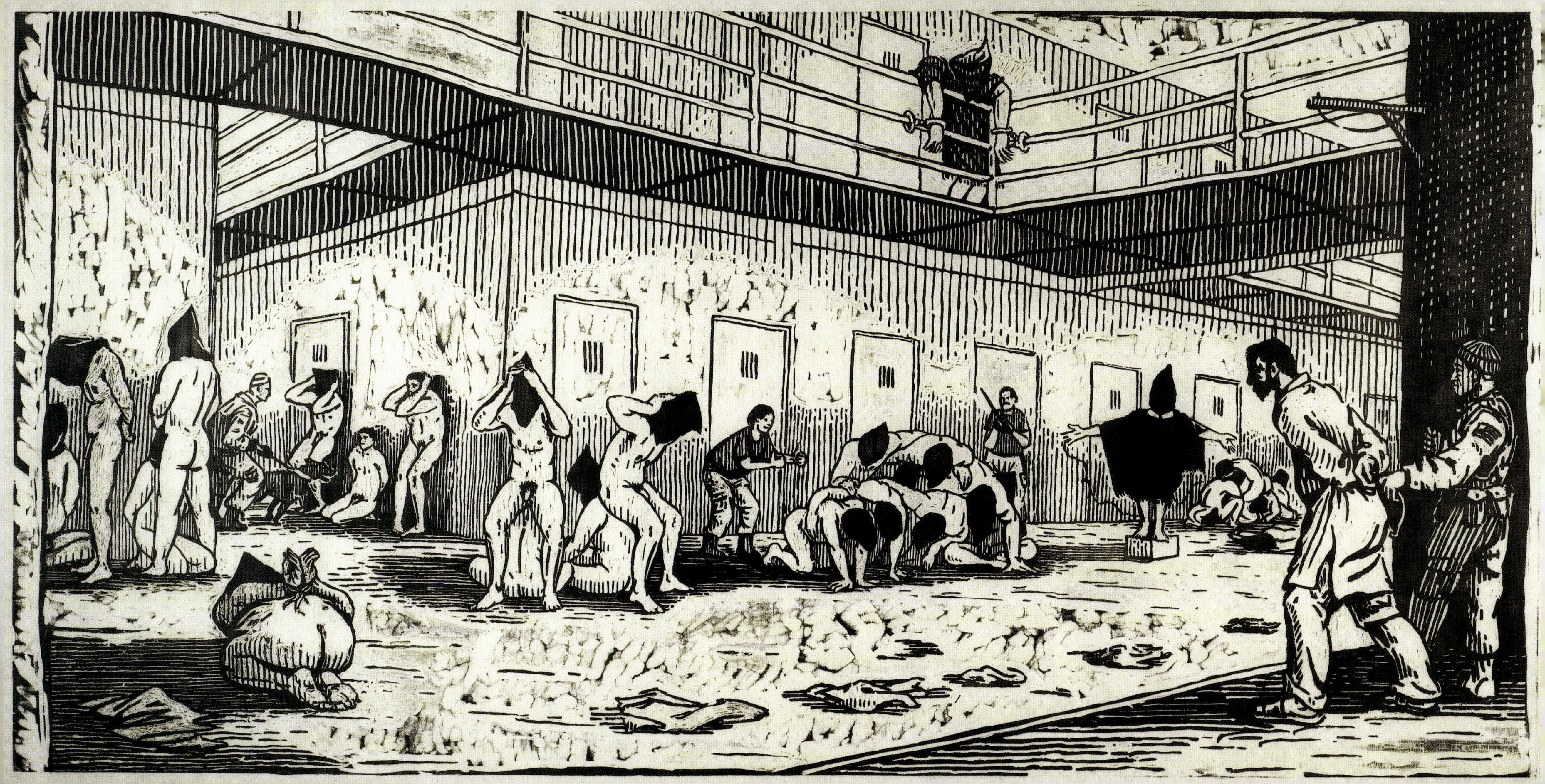

PLATE 31

Investigation

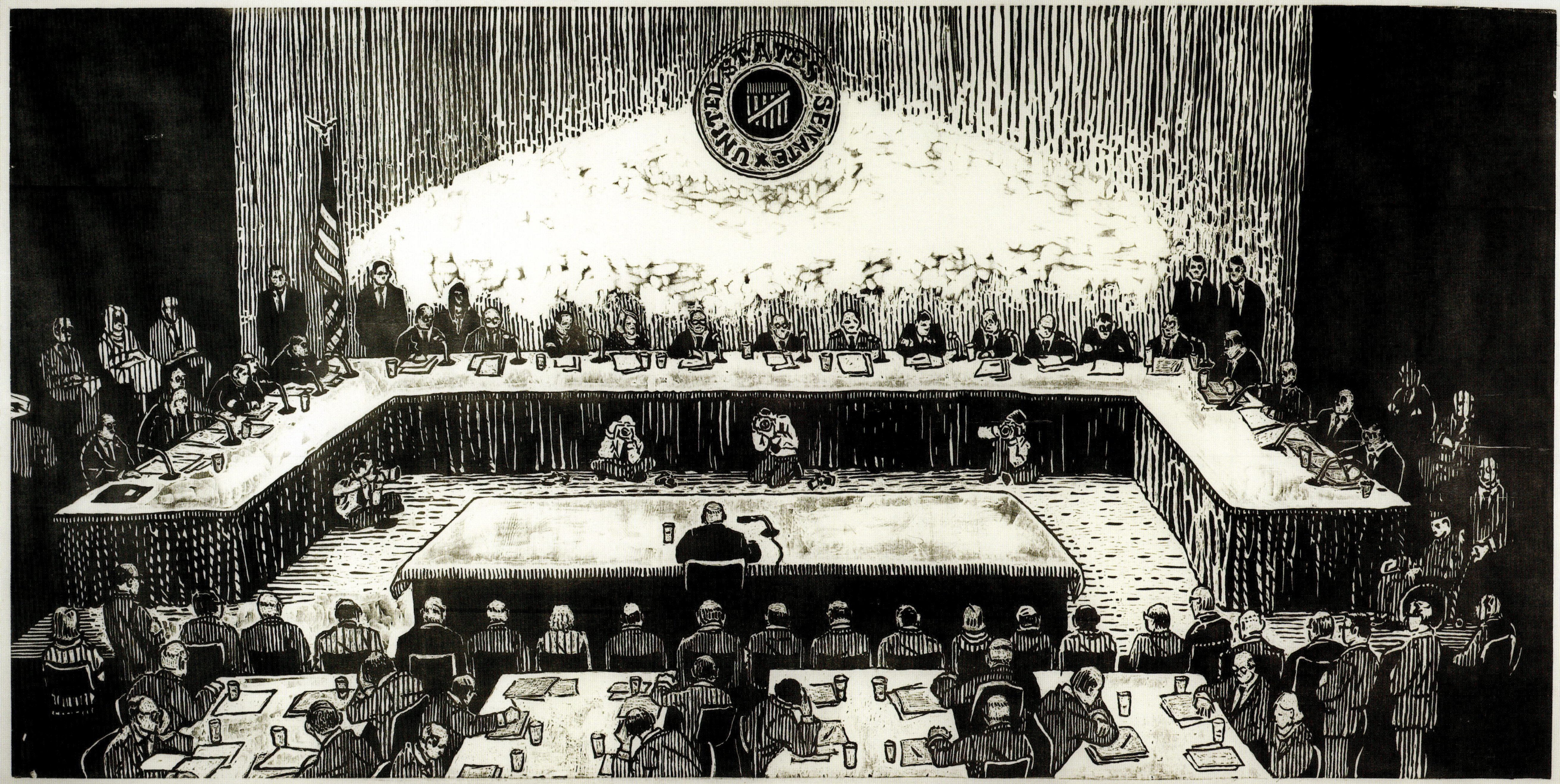
UNITED STATES SENATE

PLATE 32

Execution

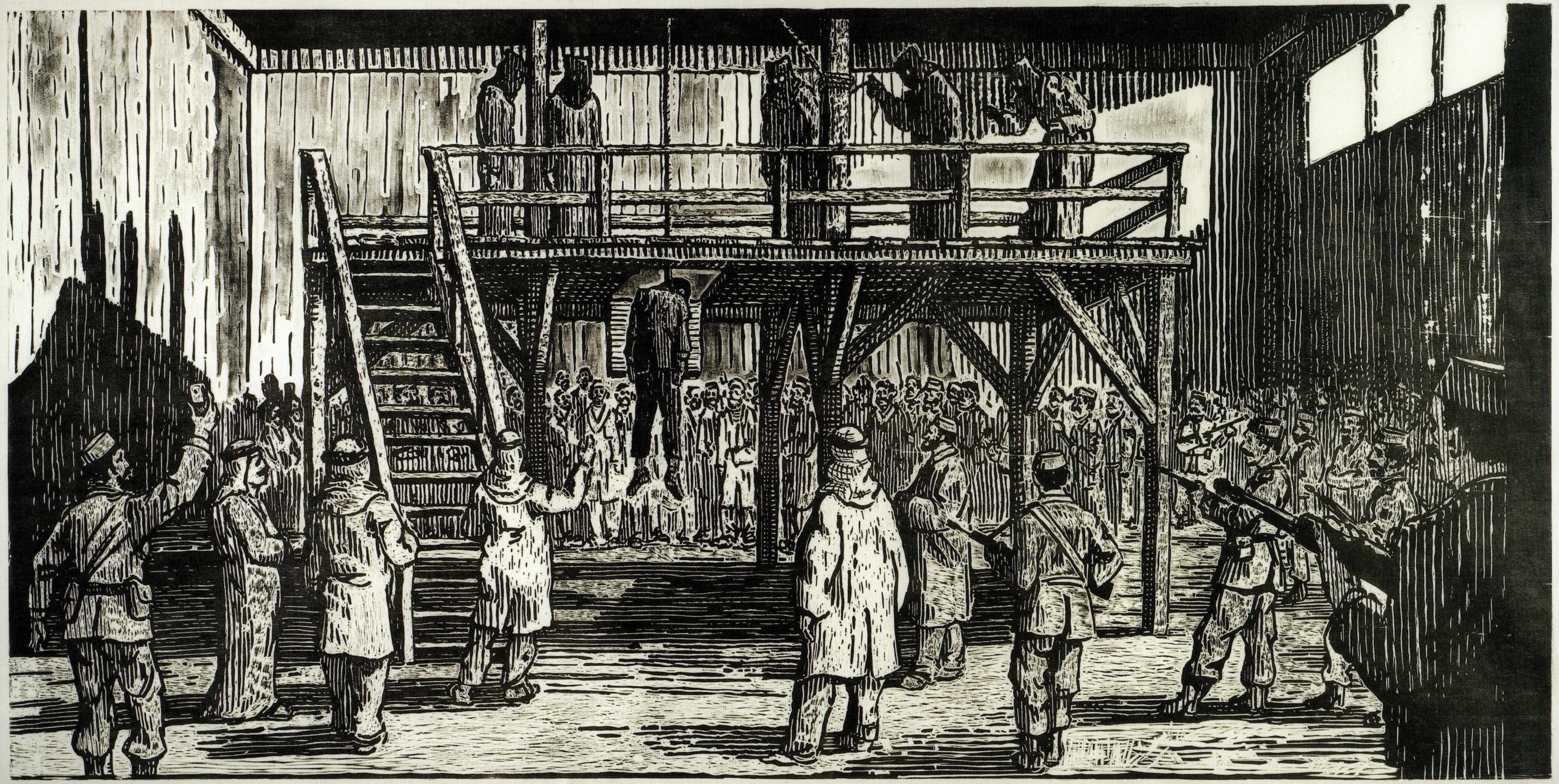

PLATE 33

Repercussion

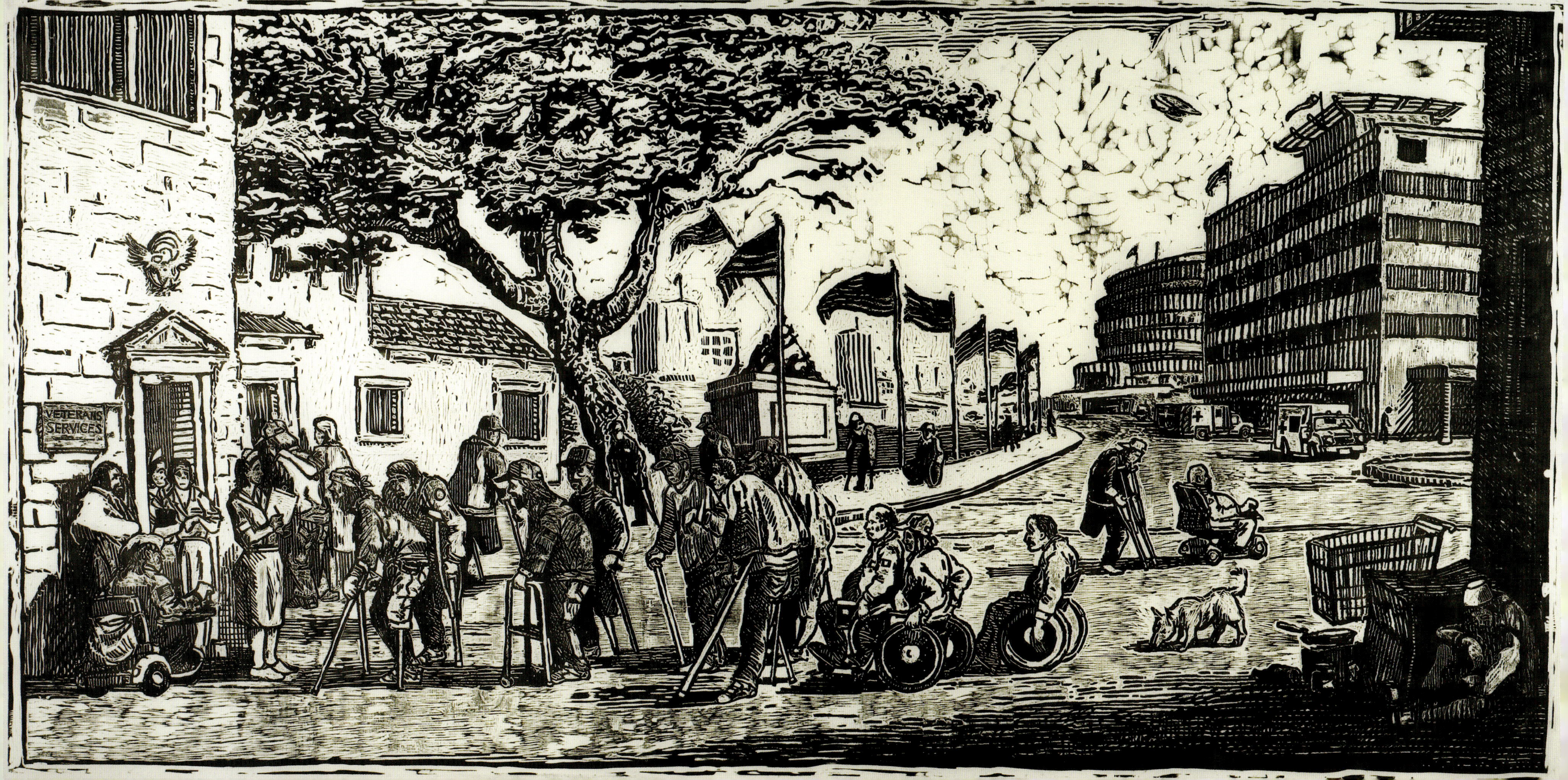
VETERANS
SERVICES

Observing Birk's Method

BY GRAHAM LARKIN, PH.D., CURATOR OF EUROPEAN AND AMERICAN ART, NATIONAL GALLERY OF CANADA

In many of his recent paintings (plates 34-42) Sandow Birk conjures up dreams and nightmares of the invasion of Iraq, in a style emulating the labored illusionism and mawkish narrative explicitness of social-realist propaganda posters or Franklin Mint plates, with strong doses of Ingres and Gérôme thrown in for good measure.[1] The fifteen woodcuts in his *The Depravities of War* series organize scenes from the same war into capriccios recalling old masters – in this case the supreme etcher Callot, interfused with the styles of later graphic masters from Piranesi to Crumb. While no less staged, the prints are far less corny than the paintings, and arguably more interesting. The interest lies partly in the sheer sensual force of the fifteen enormous sheets of ink-drenched Japanese paper. But there is also room for more rational pleasure, in the decipherment of a willfully elaborate process of production.

Birk began this series by using pen and ink to render fifteen fantasies in Callot's manner on sheets of paper measuring approximately 10 by 17 inches. Had he been satisfied to merely make a "statement" about the war, he could just have exhibited the drawings, or he could have used them as the basis for prints on the same scale. But instead (on the advice of his collaborator Elyse Pignolet) he took the drawings "and then blew them up...simply on a copy machine at Kinko's, piecemeal, and taped [them] together at 4 by 8 feet on the floor of my studio."[2]

The visit to Kinko's is a natural course for a progressive artist of Birk's generation. Punk posters designers have long favored copy machines for their affordability (zero overhead, and a few cents a page) and – crucially – for the instant image degradation through the exaggeration of contrast and the resultant breakdown of forms. Photocopying is a good way of making an image raw and unfamiliar; a radical change of scale simply intensifies the desired estrangement. "Even in blowing them up," Birk cogently explains, "they became more interesting – the sketchiness of the small-scale drawings became bolder and the gestures more apparent, the figures more 'blocky' and stylized, etc. They got better as they were expanded."[3]

The logic of displacement is carried further in the printshop at HuiPress in Maui, where Birk and his collaborators "wheatpasted the big sheet of paper onto birch plywood sheets, varnished it to seal it, and then started carving the boards right through the paper." Judging from the patchwork of pictorial effects in the final product, this operation of laying siege to 480 square feet of plywood was a relatively speedy and unruly affair, with Birk giving direction but also allowing his company of carvers to improvise in their interpretation of his blown-up pen lines. Given the enormity of the task, the decision not to micromanage the carving was doubtless an economizing measure, but it was also a way of opening up the work to further displacement. From one print to the next, the differences in the rendering of smoke or sky feel like inventive local solutions to the collective task of translating the already-degraded copy. Countless other contingencies come into play in the laborious process of assembling the huge sheets of Japanese paper, inking the blocks, and pulling the inked prints – not to mention the vagaries of storage and display.[4]

And so Birk's taste for the conditional leads to a productive logic of displacement, beginning with his delighted misrecognition of his own handiwork upon seeing it enlarged. He is inexorably engaged in a process of estrangement, as theorized by Viktor Schklovsky in his concept of *ostranenie* (making strange, defamiliarization), and by Bertolt Brecht in his concept of the *Verfremdungseffekt* (alienation effect). In his seminal 1917 essay "Art as Technique" Shklovsky argues that

> [t]he technique of art is to make objects "unfamiliar," to make forms difficult, to increase the difficulty and length of perception because the process of perception is an aesthetic end in itself and must be prolonged. Art is a way of experiencing the artfulness of an object; the object is not important.[5]

In the writing and staging of his plays Brecht used many tricks of estrangement to drive home the artificiality of the action before his audience, who would thereby avoid the Aristotelian traps of suspended disbelief and politically impotent catharsis. In analogous manner (and in stark contrast to the über-Aristotelian *Saving Private Ryan*), Birk's *Depravities* draw attention to their own constructedness through surprising beauty (mannered swirls of smoke with the blackness and viscosity of tar); through the roughly worked surface and the presence of degraded or distorted forms; through the evidence of varying styles of representation indicating multiple artists; through the stagelike arrangement of the composition; and through the self-conscious intermingling of figures based on photos of Iraq with figures adapted from Callot.

Many of these defamiliarizing ploys (staginess, stock poses, uncanny distortion, and enlargement) come together in the figures of soldiers, which we have already seen Birk describe as made "better" through exaggerated blockiness and stylization. Could it be that they are better because, in their uncanny stiffness, vagueness, and stockiness, they readily recall the 3-inch-high plastic soldiers that little boys consume by the bagful? Since their stockiness and genericism become even more pronounced through enlargement, the enormous woodcuts become thoroughly antimonumental – become mockumental, if you will. This play of scale is genuinely Callotesque, with a dash of Swift or Carroll. If Callot's little *Miseries* show the world through the wrong end of the telescope, then Birk's grandiose *Depravities* show a small drawing of tiny figures, blown up to such a size that … I must be shrinking!

The persistent memory of those 3-inch plastic figures becomes most disturbing in the scenes of *Degradation* and *Humiliation*, where the dinky Lynndie England and friends take childlike pleasure in dumping out piles of faceless enemy soldiers and arranging them into scenes of obsessive order or picturesque disarray. Let's face it: this primal pleasure is familiar to all little boys, and evidently to some girls. Our leaders decry this child's play as abnormal, but wouldn't it be truer to see it as the origin of all war?

1 I am grateful to Sandow Birk and Paul Mullowney for providing me with information and proofs. Thanks also to Geoff Morrow for his wise and timely advice.

2 E-mail to the author, July 5, 2007. In the same e-mail Birk notes that "Elyse Pignolet...suggested that rather than doing small prints based on small prints, we could do huge prints based on small prints as a way of adding another tweak to the Callots, or of being more grandiose and more theatrical and bolder and pushing it farther."

3 Ibid.

4 Aside from reproductions, the only works from the series I had seen, upon writing this, were advanced proofs of *Occupation* and *Detention*, which I was able to view at the National Gallery of Canada thanks to a large table that could support one print plus a viewer or two. The printer, Paul Mullowney of HuiPress, informs me that to display the works he is "simply going to be putting hinges on the back which hold velcro tabs and then [suspending each work] on the wall." (E-mail to the author, 5 July 2007.)

5 Viktor Shklovsky, "Art as Technique," in *Theory of Prose*, trans. Benjamin Sher (Elmwoodark: Dalkey Archive Press, 1990), p. 12.

SANDOW BIRK

Selected Paintings

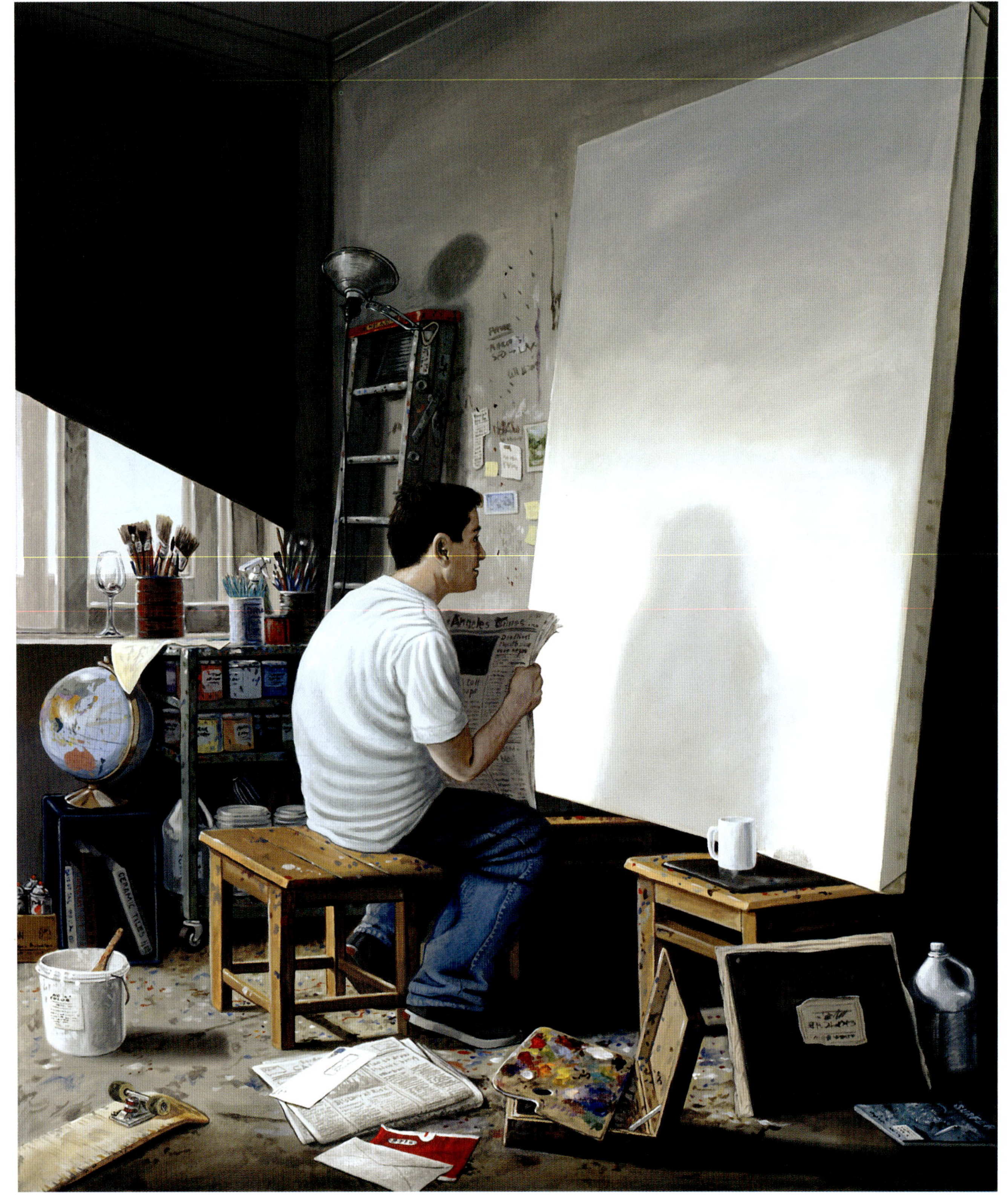

PLATE 34

In Days of War
2006
oil and acrylic on canvas
32" x 28"

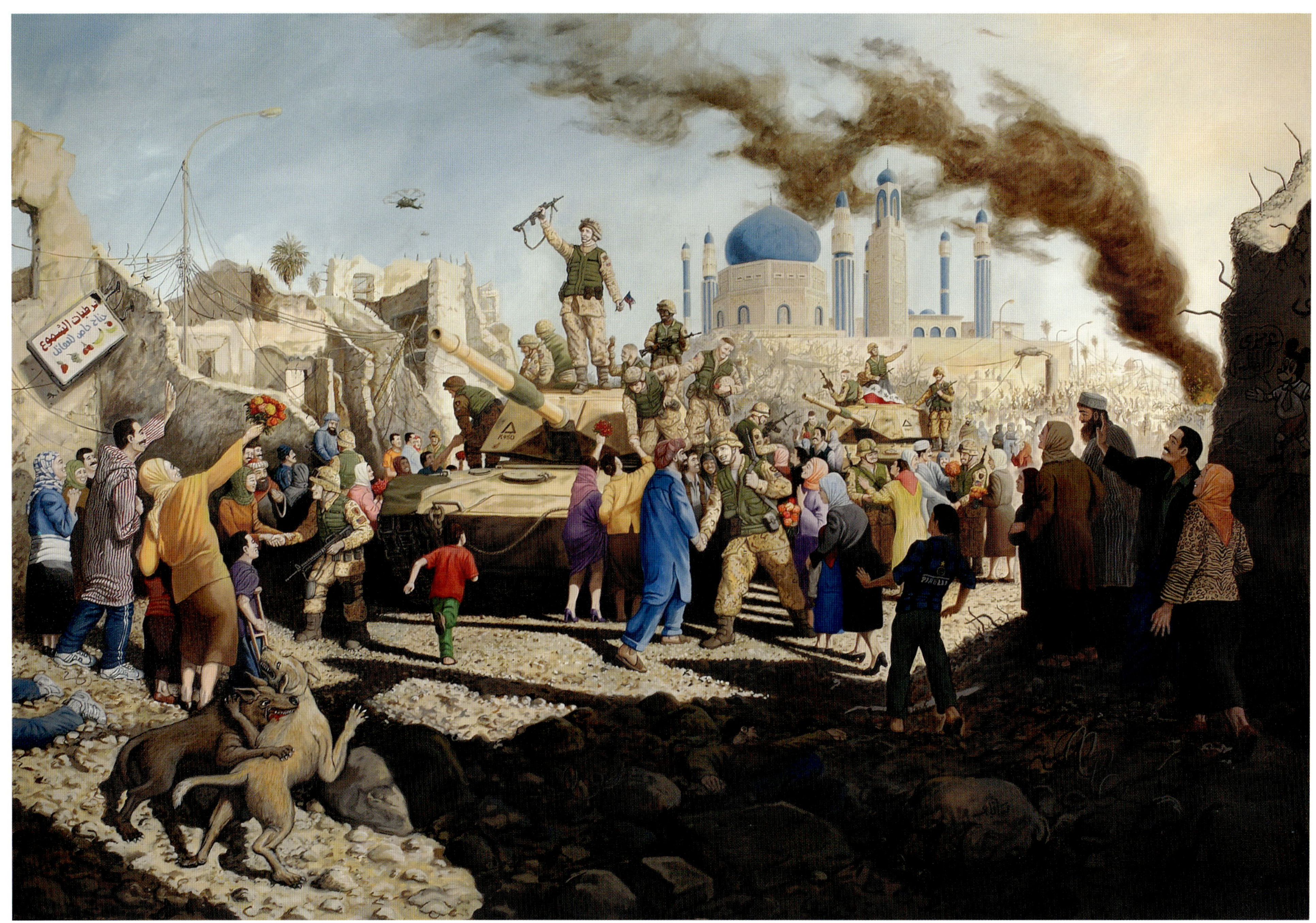

PLATE 35

The Liberation of Baghdad
2006
oil and acrylic on canvas
62" x 96"

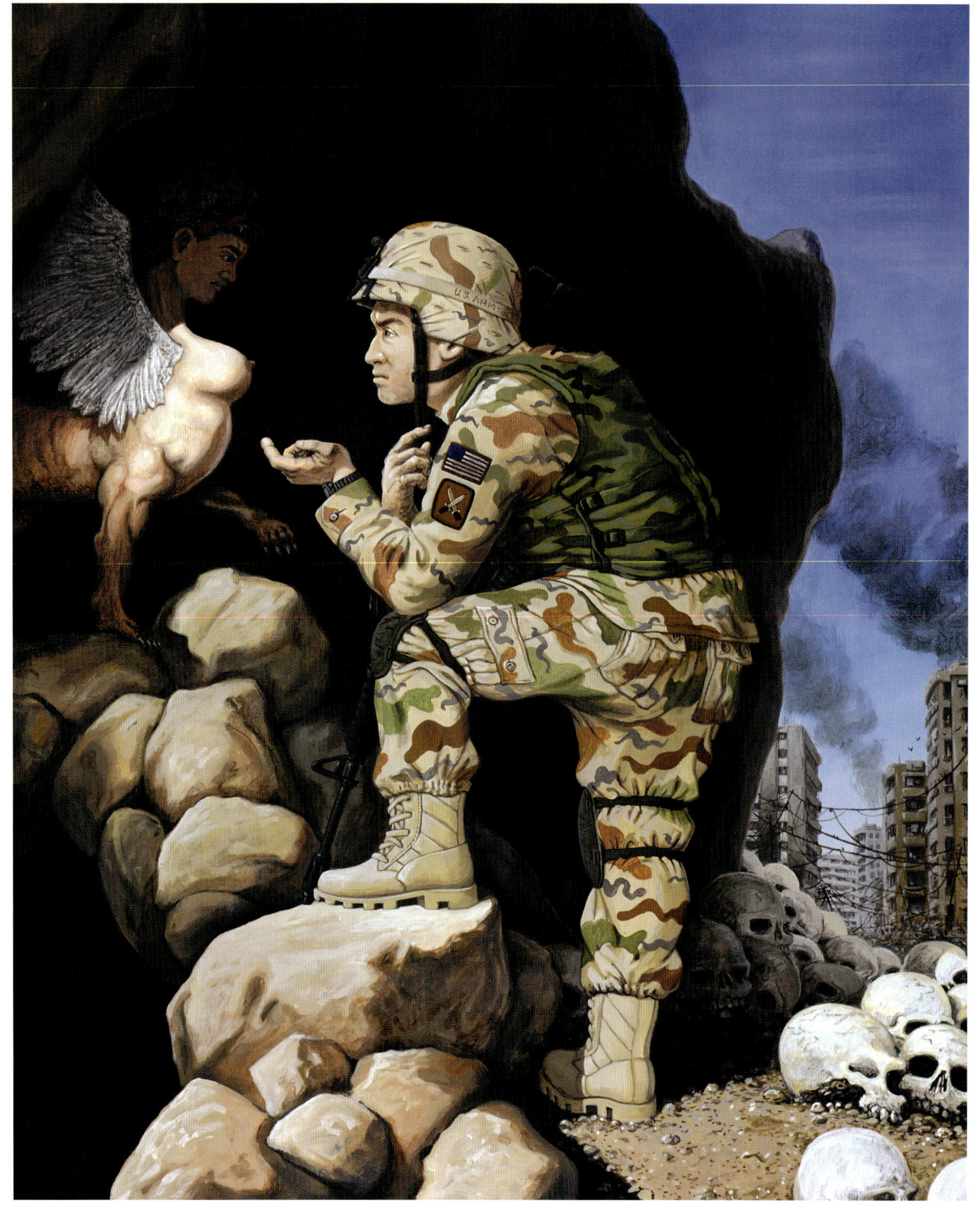

PLATE 36

The Riddle of the Sphynx
2007
oil and acrylic on canvas
30" x 24"

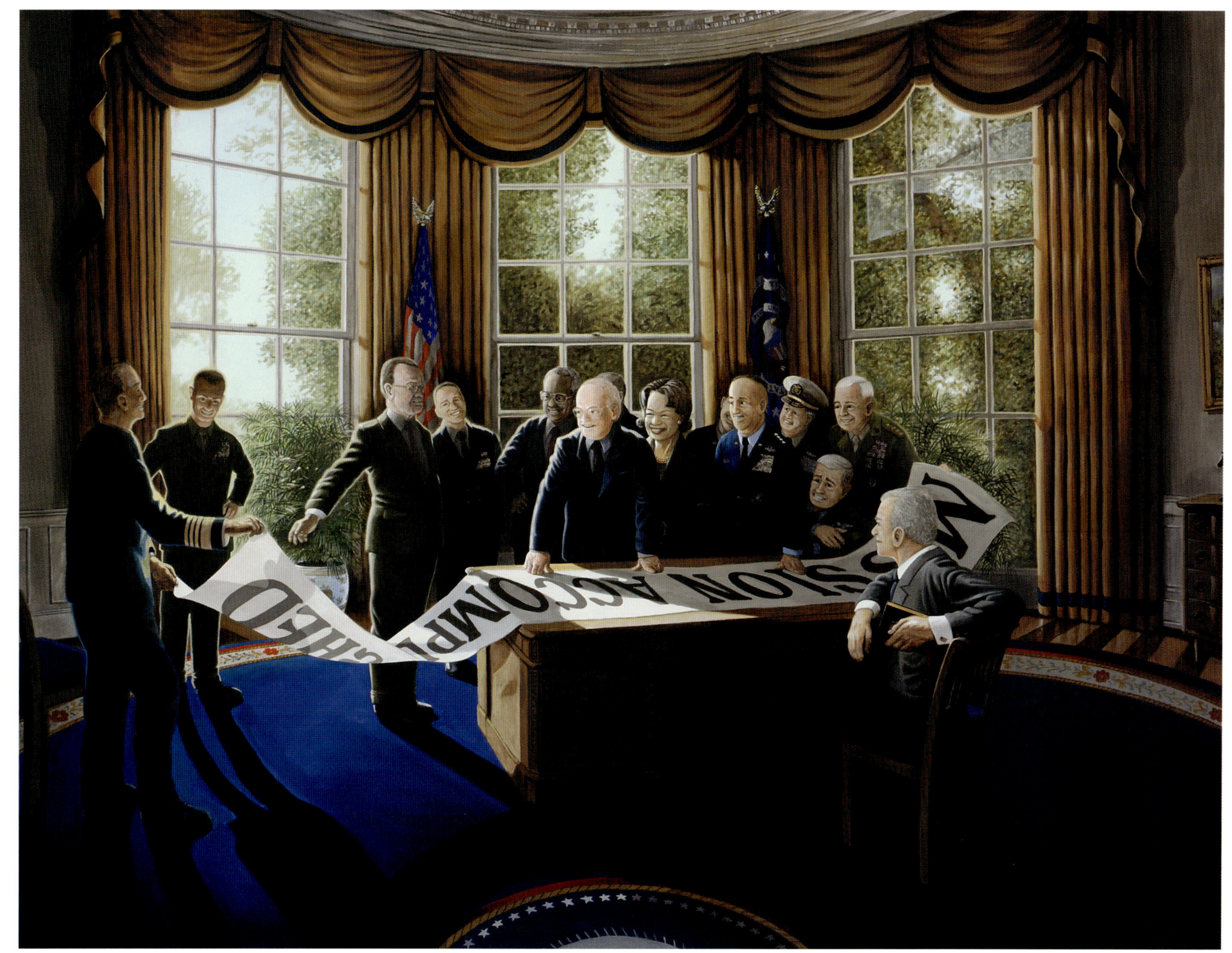

PLATE 37

Secretary of State Donald Rumsfeld Presenting His Plan for the Invasion of Iraq
2006
oil and acrylic on canvas
54" x 68"

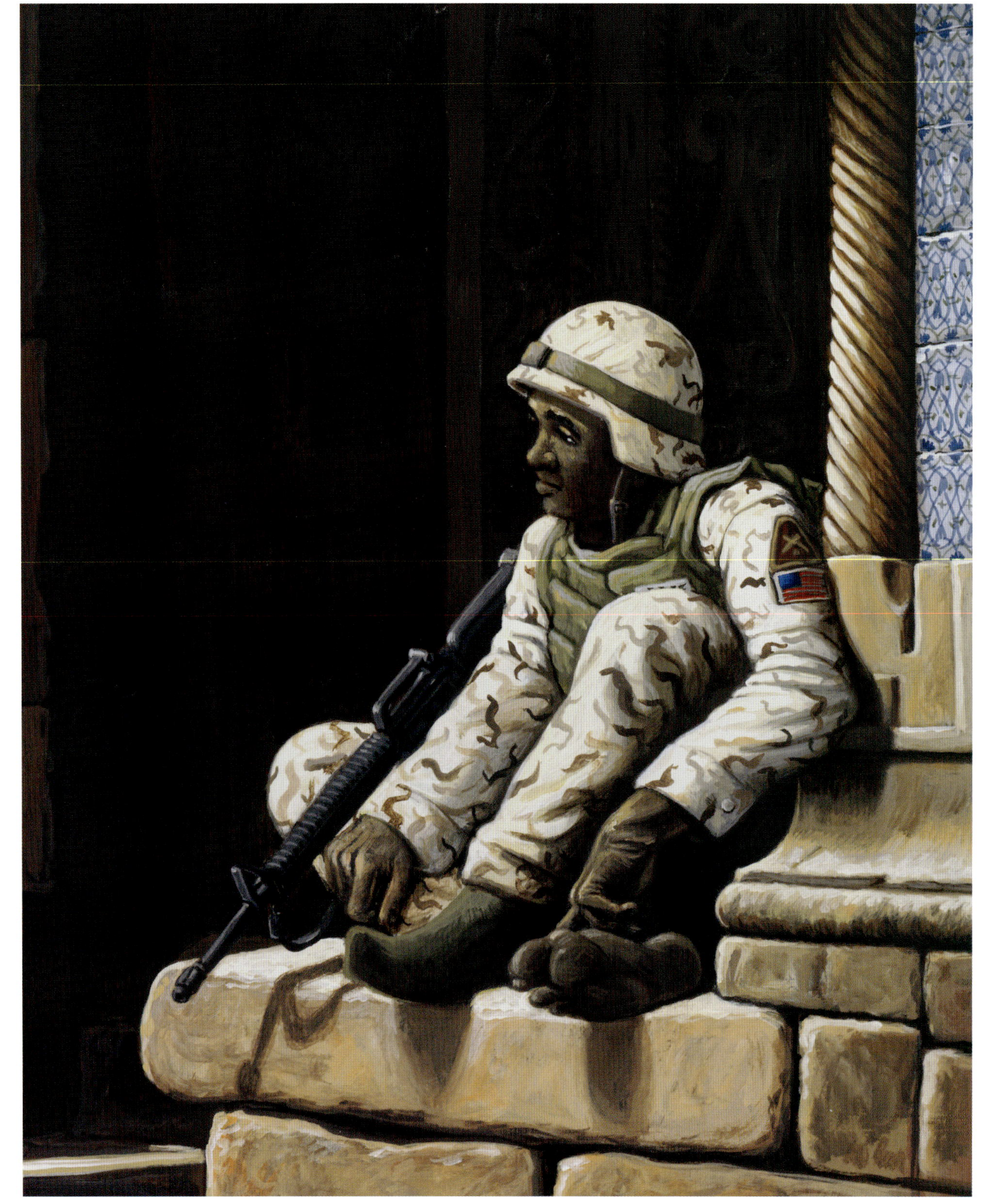

PLATE 38

Hero
2007
oil and acrylic on masonite
10" x 8"

PLATE 39

البطل

2007
oil and acrylic on masonite
10" x 8"

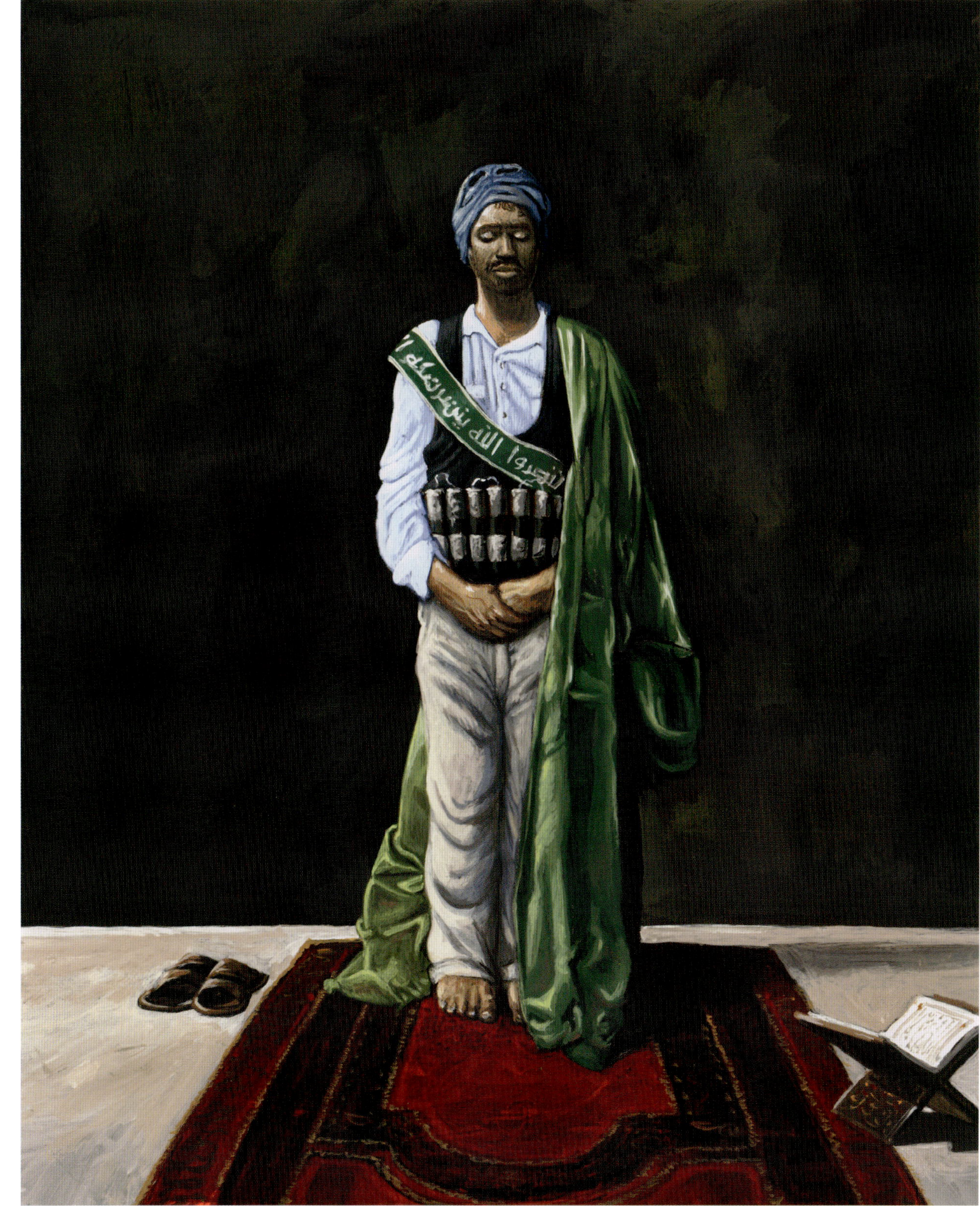

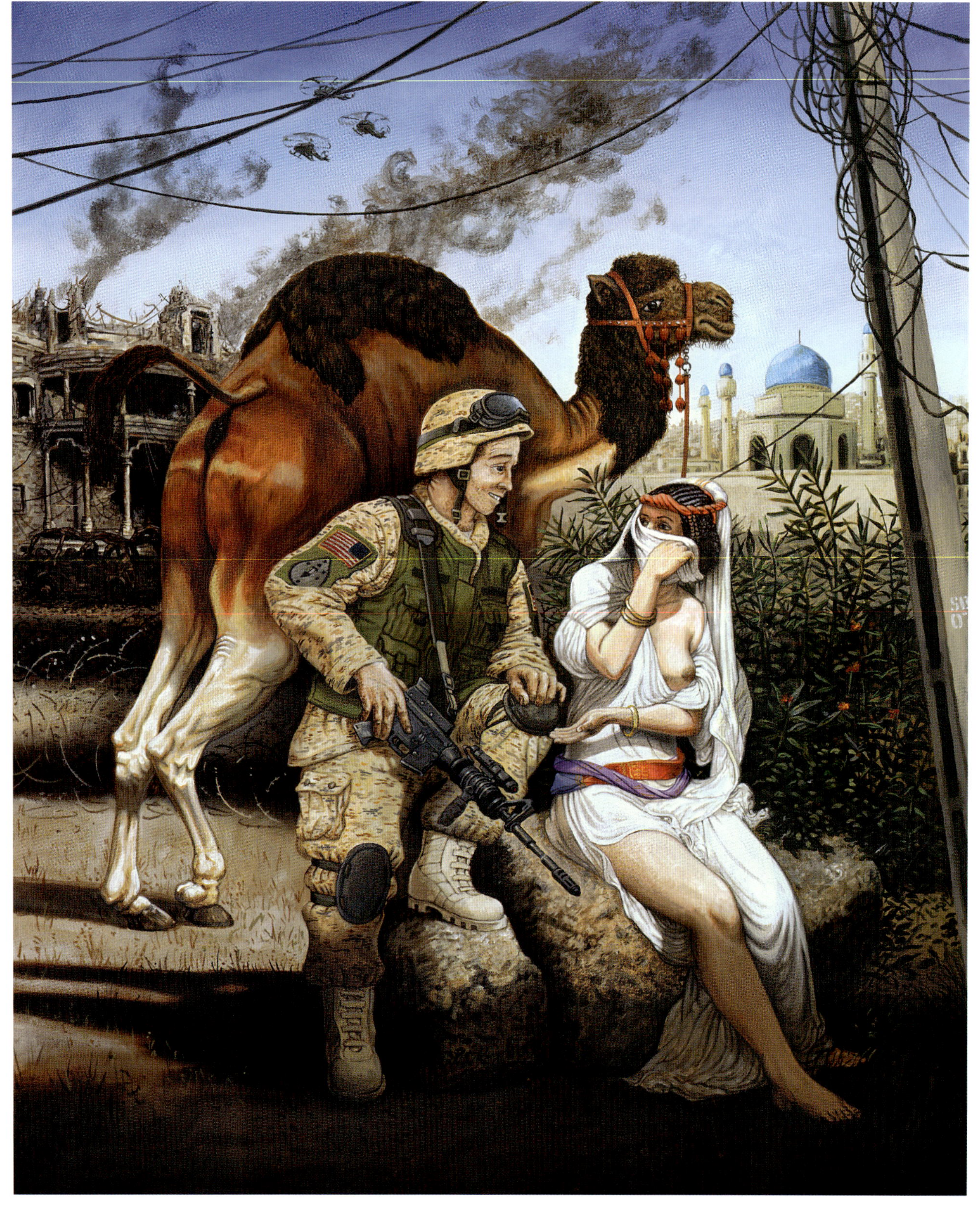

PLATE 40

The Soldier's Dream
2007
oil and acrylic on canvas
30" x 24"

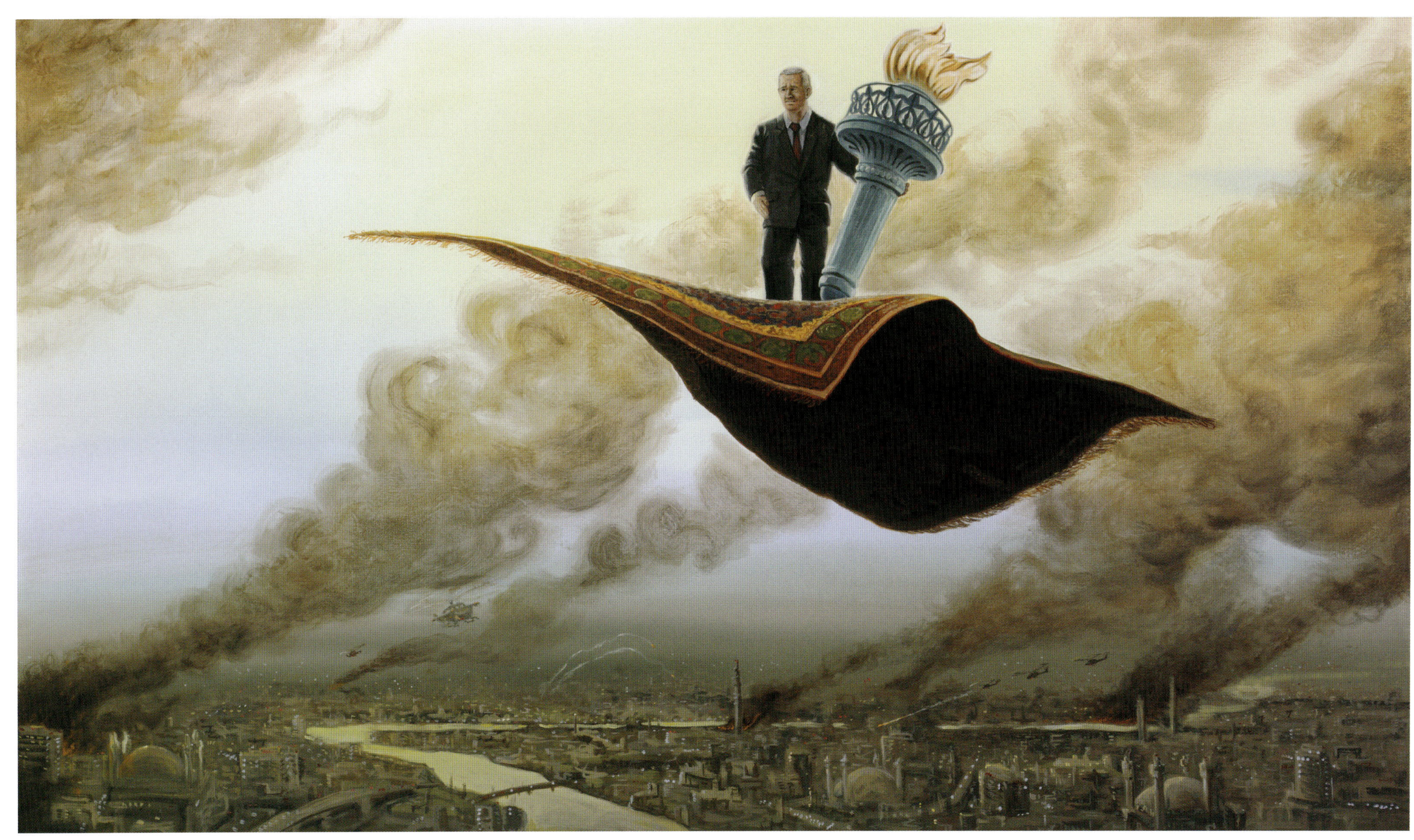

PLATE 41

The President's Dream
2007
oil and acrylic on canvas
28" x 48"

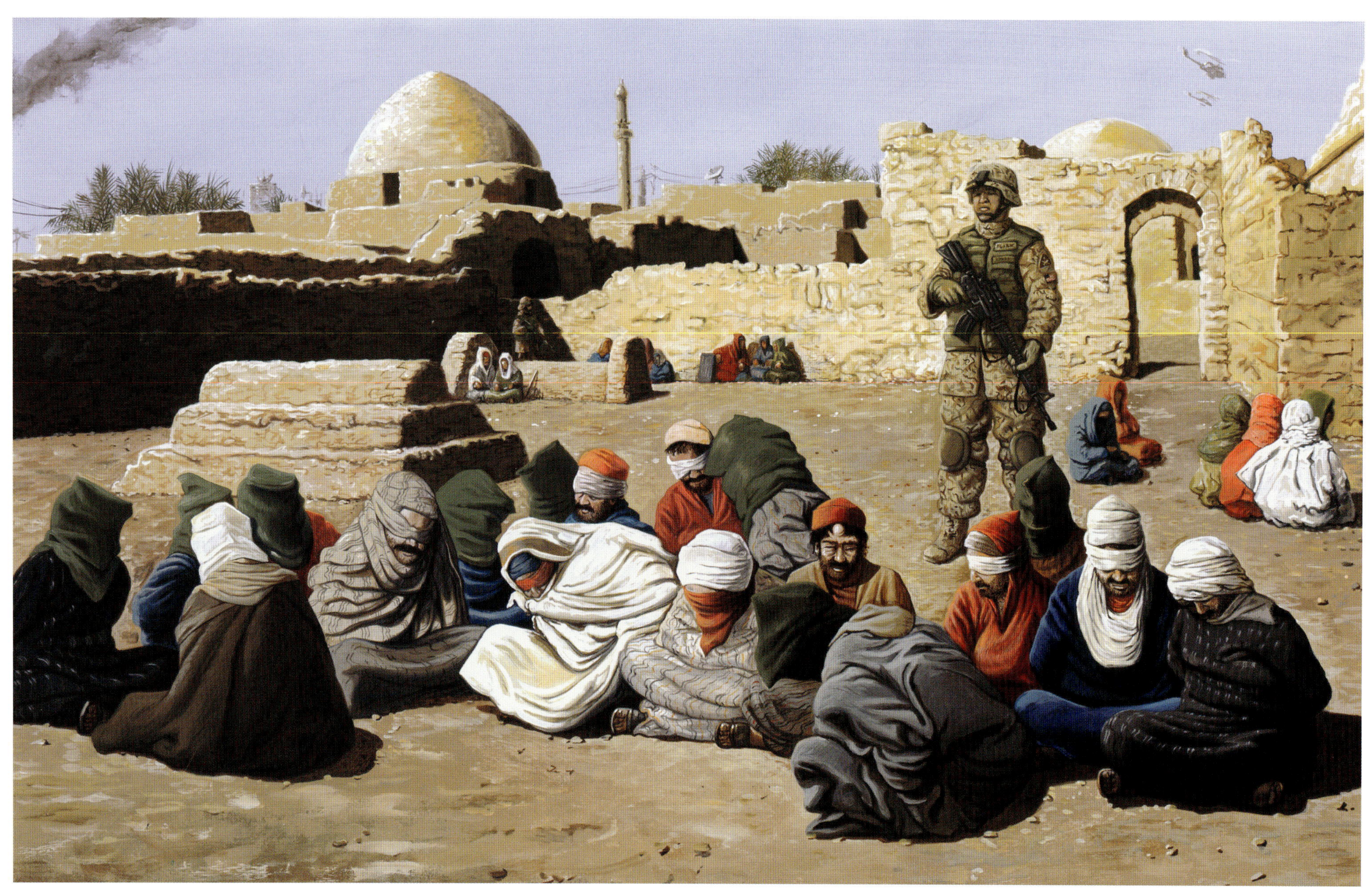

PLATE 42

Village Scene, Afghanistan
2007
oil and acrylic on canvas
22" x 34"

The Politics of Landscape

by Catharine Clark, Director, Catharine Clark Gallery, San Francisco

On a recent drive from San Francisco on US 101 to Los Angeles, I thought about how much Sandow Birk's artworks are quintessentially about landscape. Not *plein air* painting or formal studies on natural beauty, but about the romantic tradition of landscape painting and the politics embedded in classical landscape renderings in which the promise of beauty means politics packaged in an often idealized view of the natural world. California's landscape offers this duality: extreme physical beauty, wealth, abundant farmland, mountains, and beaches – punctuated by prisons, military bases, the homeless, graffiti, fast-food establishments, and signs of environmental trouble. It is a region of social, political, religious, and cultural extremes and contradictions. It promises the American Dream for its citizens and newly arriving immigrants and delivers the harsh reality of high living expenses, unchecked development, polluted beaches, and drug-infested communities for many of its inhabitants. Sandow Birk has lived in this environment since the 1960s, and it is often the subject of his art.

I first met Sandow Birk in 1993 after a painting of his was reproduced in *Visions Art Quarterly*. I was drawn to his work because he uses classical painting and art-historical references to reflect on current environmental, political, and cultural landscapes. For example, in *Death of Manuel* (1992), Birk portrayed the gang violence of his Los Angeles neighborhood, borrowing the composition of *The Death of Marat* by eighteenth-century French painter Jacques-Louis David (1748-1825). Similarly, in *Aggro Crowd at Lower Trestles (Watson and the Shark)* (1990), he appropriated John Singleton Copley's *Watson and The Shark* (1778) to convey the Pacific surf and the environmental problems lurking therein.

Among the first of Birk's projects I exhibited was the product of a collaboration he initiated with graffiti artists and other members of his community. He invited the youths to "tag" blank canvases, creating a backdrop or landscape on which Birk rendered scenes of abject poverty and disenfranchised Los Angelenos. Spending time in San Francisco for his exhibitions at the Catharine Clark Gallery, Birk was made more aware of the intense rivalry between San Francisco and Los Angeles. As he contemplated a possible move to San Francisco, he began a series of satirical works collectively titled *In Smog and Thunder: The Great War of the Californias*. The fictitious battles of these paintings are set on the beaches, in the ocean, and within the cities and towns that make up this most populous state in the nation. The paintings appropriate the compositions of historical war genres and maritime paintings, such as Albrecht Altdorfer's *Battle of Alexander* (1529) and James Edward Buttersworth's *Clipper Dreadnought* (c. 1853). In the *Smog and Thunder* series, generals and lieutenants reflect the diversity of California's population, and rather than perched on horses they ride Ducati or Harley Davidson motorcycles or balance on surfboards at Fort Point under the Golden Gate Bridge. Sculptures in the form of ships look uncannily like the Getty Museum and the San Francisco Museum of Modern Art. Military helicopters and jets are assembled from trash collected on the beaches, and sponsorship of the war is "brought to the viewer" by major multinational corporations and media conglomerates such as NBC and Sony, whose logos are branded on the ships and planes. As in many wars, it is difficult to comprehend who is winning. But whoever is to be victorious hardly matters because it is subtly made clear that the battles are being fought in part over water rights. Such rights are a persistent problem for all Californians as we periodically face drought and water shortage with no end in sight to the ever-growing population that further stresses the precious resource. Pictured in one of the series' closing works, *Rendezvous at Twin Peaks (The Battle of San Francisco)* (1996), are lawyers and movie producers negotiating film rights to portray *The Great War of the Californias* as a blockbuster, all while enjoying the fare from a mobile taco stand atop Twin Peaks.

The transition from *In Smog and Thunder* to *Prisonation* seemed a natural one for Birk. After all, examination of water politics in California turned up lots of other data about life in the state. Apparently there are more people incarcerated per capita in California than in any other state in the nation. The 33 California state prisons are grossly overpopulated, and laws such as the notorious "three strikes" mean that even minor convictions can result in a lifetime of imprisonment. For the *Prisonation* project, Sandow chose nineteenth-century California landscape painting as the rubric for presenting each of the prisons within an idyllic landscape. Similar to the thesis presented in *West As America: Reinterpreting Images of the Frontier, 1820-1920* at the National Museum of American Art, whose curator, William Truettner, and team of scholars, seem to courageously argue, through paintings that document how frontier images define our ideas about our national past, that many nineteenth-century landscape painters, such as Frederic Church, Thomas Hill, and William Keith, were propagandists for the westward expansion of America, Birk approaches the rendering of the prisons in such landscapes to show another consequence of Manifest Destiny – prison building as a growth industry.

Nineteenth-century California landscape painters rendered idealized images of the Western region in part to "sell" the area to the population in the rest of the nation – Manifest Destiny was in full play. Birk uses the visual seduction of beautifully rendered California landscapes to simultaneously reveal and hide a darker story about the American Dream in the West – interaction with the landscape is denied to an increasing portion of the state's population.

From California prisons to Dante Alighieri's *The Divine Comedy* might seem like a leap in Birk's conceptual continuity until one recalls that *The Divine Comedy* is a fourteenth-century epic poem in which Dante travels through the landscapes of Hell and Purgatory guided by Virgil, and through Paradise led by his love, Beatrice, traversing the map from the lowest circle of Hell to Heaven. The story is a critique of what Dante considered unjust control by the Pope over Florence. In Sandow Birk and Marcus Sanders' modernized version of *The Divine Comedy*, Dante's original story is made accessible through the use of contemporary language. (Dante is credited with being the first to author a book in vernacular language, making his writing accessible to a wider readership.) Birk and Sanders, like Dante, also populate their poem with contemporary political and religious characters, which helps to elucidate the significance, for the modern reader, of Dante's characters. For his images in *The Divine Comedy*, Birk uses Gustave Doré's engravings as a visual template, updating the compositions with contemporary city scenes, landscapes, monuments, and buildings to make us aware that the complexity and corruption of religion and politics are age-old concerns. The landscapes of hell, purgatory, and heaven are mapped and traversed by the same historic characters (Dante, Virgil and Beatrice), but Birk uses the biblical topographies as metaphors, showing us that the real concerns are the plight of politics, culture, and the environment here on earth today.

Since Birk's work often reflects current political issues, it is no surprise that he has embarked upon a project titled *The Depravities of War*, the subject of the exhibition documented by this catalog. Based on the series of etchings by French artist Jacques Callot (1592-1635) titled *The Miseries of War*, Birk's *Depravities of War* series comprises fifteen 4-by-8-foot woodcuts and a suite of accompanying drawings that served as the studies for the woodcuts. The project is complemented by several large-scale paintings – epic, colorful versions of the *Depravities* woodcuts – that are based compositionally on paintings about the glories of war from Napoleon's time and images from Russian socialist battlefield paintings. The *Depravities of War* project includes scenes of people enlisting, heading to boot camp and training camps, leaving for war, invading Iraq, and liberating Baghdad. It also contains images of Abu Ghraib, the U.S. Senate hearings, and the execution of Saddam Hussein. Like so much of Birk's work, this project explores the disparity between what our government promises and what in fact occurs. Birk consistently argues in his work that history has apparently taught us little. We are particularly aware of this now, with the war in Iraq, and we are especially in need of this body of work at this time.

The Iraq war is about the control of landscape – its oil fields and other natural resources – and about who ultimately will govern it. It is also about religion – the Islamic Jihadist and the Christian soldier – and whose will is more supported by God. It is about an expanded version of Manifest Destiny cloaked in terminology about Democracy, which seems to be taking the form of a new colonialism, a kind-of exported Jim Crowism.

Having exhibited Sandow's work since 1994, I am consistently impressed by the scope of his approach to a subject. No concept seems too large to tackle, and often, as in Dante's *Divine Comedy* or Hollywood horror films, the exhibitions have sequels because the content expands beyond one show's worth of material and the stories extend in time. Sandow's approach to storytelling encompasses all media. Drawings, prints, paintings, sets, sculptures, murals, film, audio, and written texts are all forms he uses to elucidate a narrative. The one device that has remained consistent is his use of history to shed light on the present. This perhaps reveals his classical training in Paris, France, and in Bath, England, his education at Otis in Los Angeles, and his upbringing on the beaches of Southern California.

Returning to my drive on US 101 through California, I remark how the topography of California, like Sandow's lofty concepts executed with accessible imagery, is a hybrid of highbrow and lowbrow cultural elements. Hearst Castle and Italian Tuscan-style McMansions seek to reproduce an idea of opulence and wealth inherited from Europe, yet they are juxtaposed with drive-thru fast food chains and other displays of our convenience-oriented culture that are quintessentially American. The question plaguing me now about Sandow's work is, what's next? To answer that could predict the next disaster that will befall this land, or it might be the needed reminder to insist on a brighter future – a goal that is within the grasp of us all. Given the prescience of Birk's earlier work, we should look at his art as we might at a crystal ball and heed the message therein.

PLATE 43

Map of Purgatory
2003
ink on mylar
10" x 8"

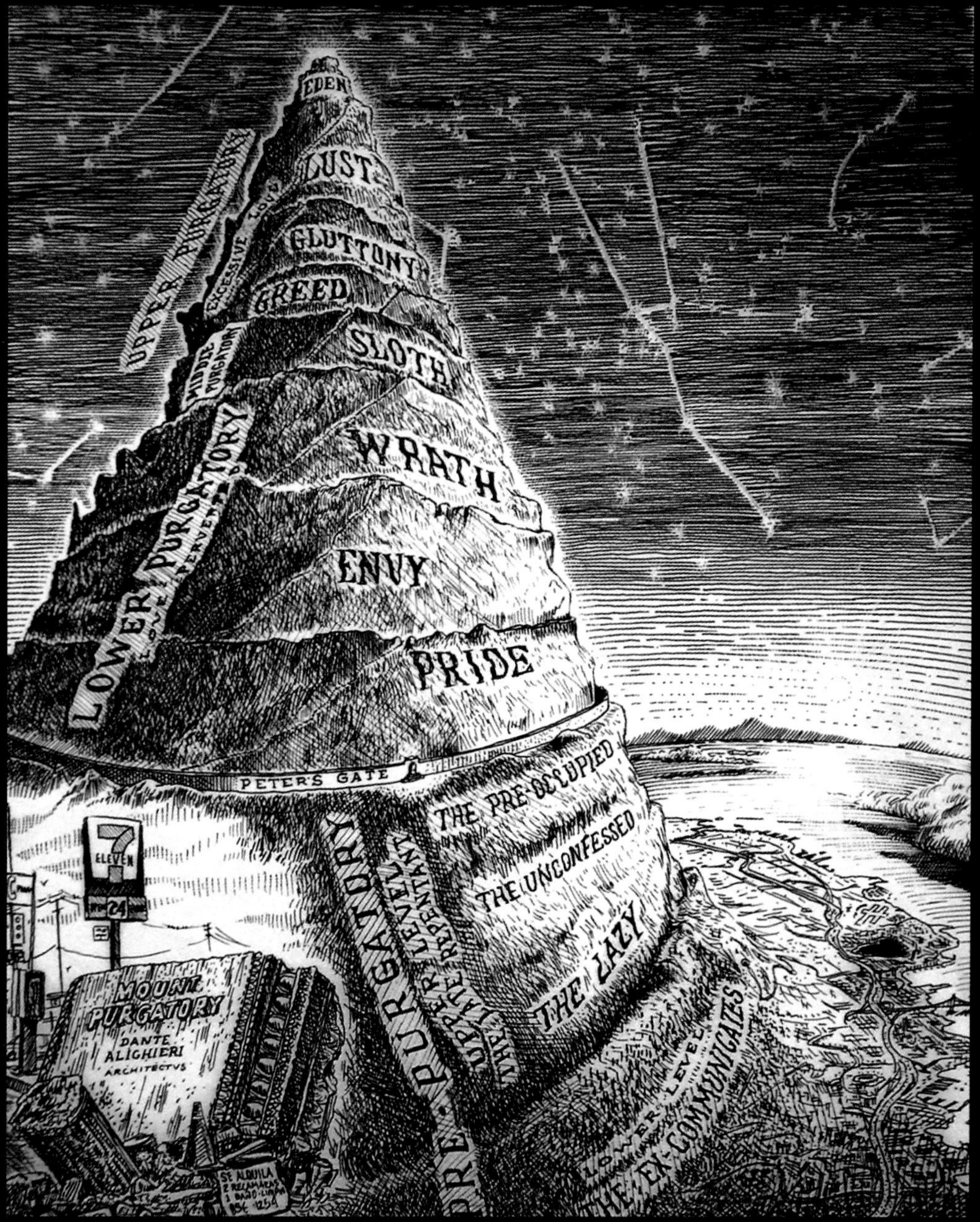

Sandow Birk

Raised on the beaches of California and currently living and working in Los Angeles, Sandow Birk is well traveled and a graduate of the Otis Art Institute of Parsons School of Design (presently known as Otis College of Art and Design). His work has dealt with contemporary life in its entirety. With an emphasis on social issues, frequent themes of his past work have included inner city violence, graffiti, various political issues, travel, prisons, surfing and skateboarding. He was a recipient of an NEA International Travel Grant to Mexico City in 1995, a Guggenheim Fellowship in 1996, and a Fulbright Fellowship to Rio de Janeiro for 1997. In 1999 he was awarded a Getty Fellowship for painting, followed by a City of Los Angeles (COLA) Fellowship in 2001. Sandow is represented by the Koplin del Rio Gallery in Los Angeles, Catharine Clark Gallery in San Francisco, and P.P.O.W. Gallery in New York City. Sandow's epic, pseudohistorical series *In Smog and Thunder* – in which Los Angeles and San Francisco wage all-out war for control of the Golden State – was shown at the Laguna Art Museum in 2000, and his "mockumentary" film of the same name has won numerous awards at film festivals across the country. *Prisonation*, his series of idyllic landscape paintings of prisons, was exhibited at the Santa Barbara Contemporary Arts Forum in 2001 and in New York in 2002. Most recently, Birk has completed an enormous project that involved illustrating, and rewriting in American English (with Marcus Sanders), Dante's entire *Divine Comedy*. The resulting exhibition, *Sandow Birk's Divine Comedy*, was shown at the San Jose Museum of Art in 2005 and traveled to several institutions. He has just completed a feature film, *Dante's Inferno*, in collaboration with Paul Zaloom, Sean Meredith, and Elyse Pignolet, which won numerous awards at film festivals in 2007 and is scheduled for release in 2008. He has also been awarded a Fellowship at the Smithsonian Institution's National Museum of American Art in Washington D.C., for 2007.

"Birk is pursuing one of the most fascinating, unpredictable careers in Los Angeles art." — NEW TIMES LOS ANGELES

"Sandow Birk emerges from the same just-left-of-the-mainstream school that bred [other] latter-day artists and he offers a further testament to the insight, intelligence and wit with which the post-baby boomer generation is utilizing its pop-culture saturation." — LA WEEKLY

"This version of the The Inferno *is God's face in a Groucho mask, a triumphant cathedral that will bring new readers to Dante . . . and new converts to the growing church of Sandow Birk."* — SAN FRANCISCO CHRONICLE

"Birk has got at the parts of L.A. that recall Piranesi, not David Hockney, the sinister noir terrain of freeway overpasses and cuttings and drainage ditches that create a stacked-up, tangled vertical landscape far from the flat, sunshiny L.A. of the usual iconography." — LONDON REVIEW OF BOOKS

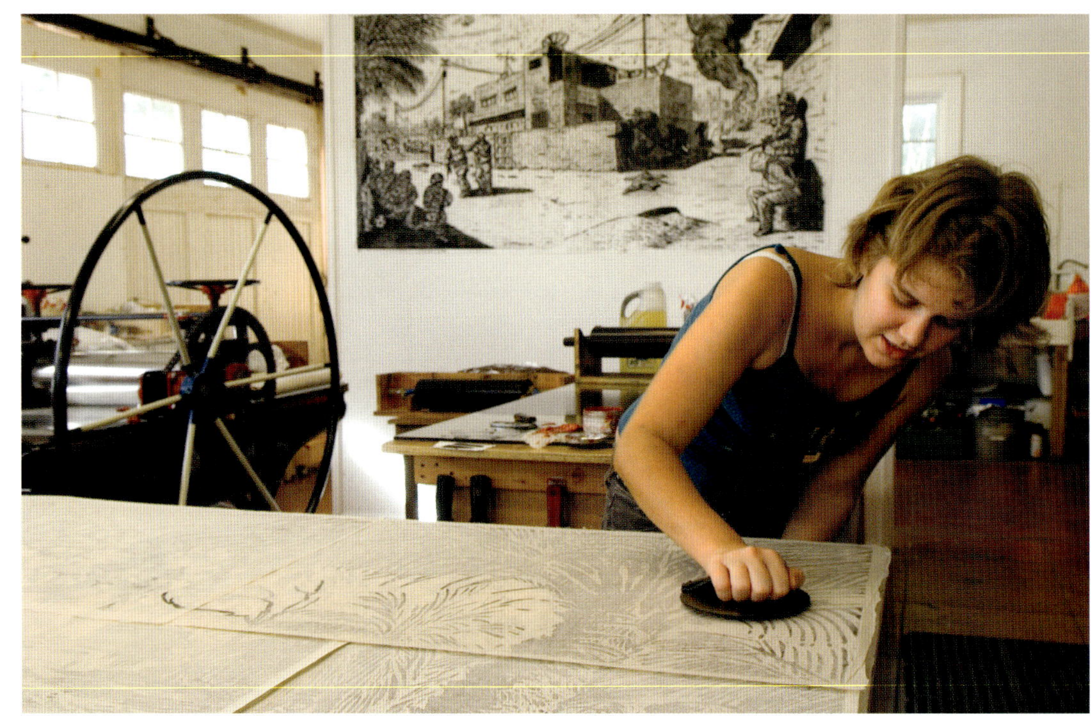

Casey Neumann

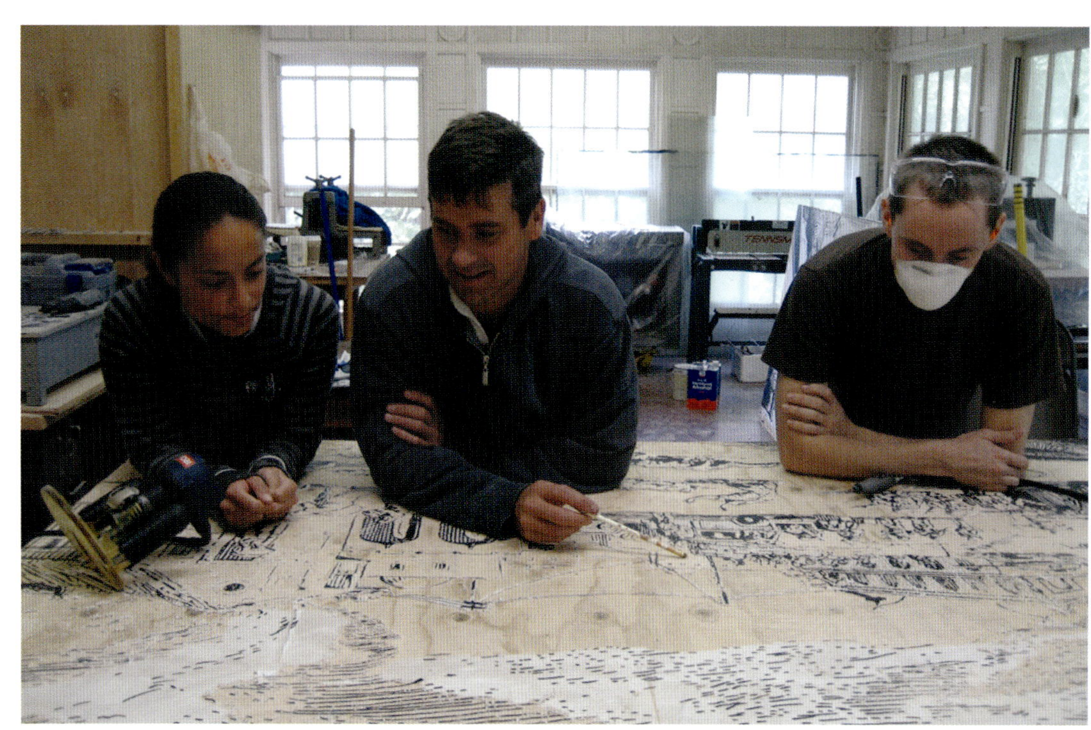

Elyse Pignolet, Sandow Birk, Samuel Carr-Prindle

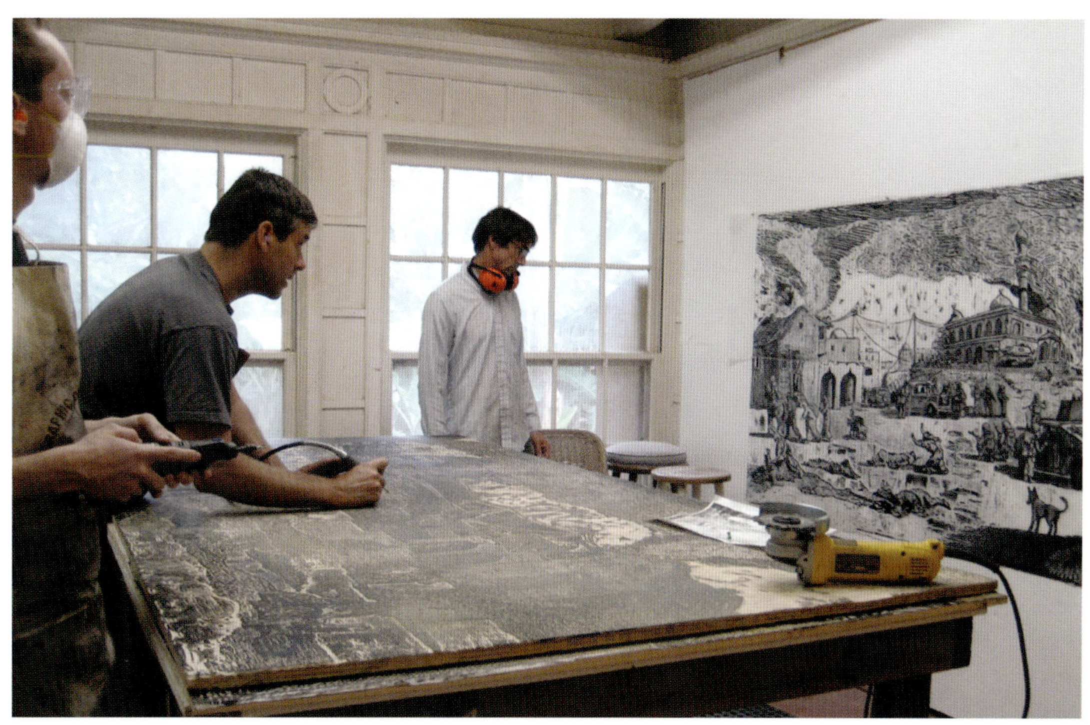

Samuel Carr-Prindle, Sandow Birk, Paul Mullowney

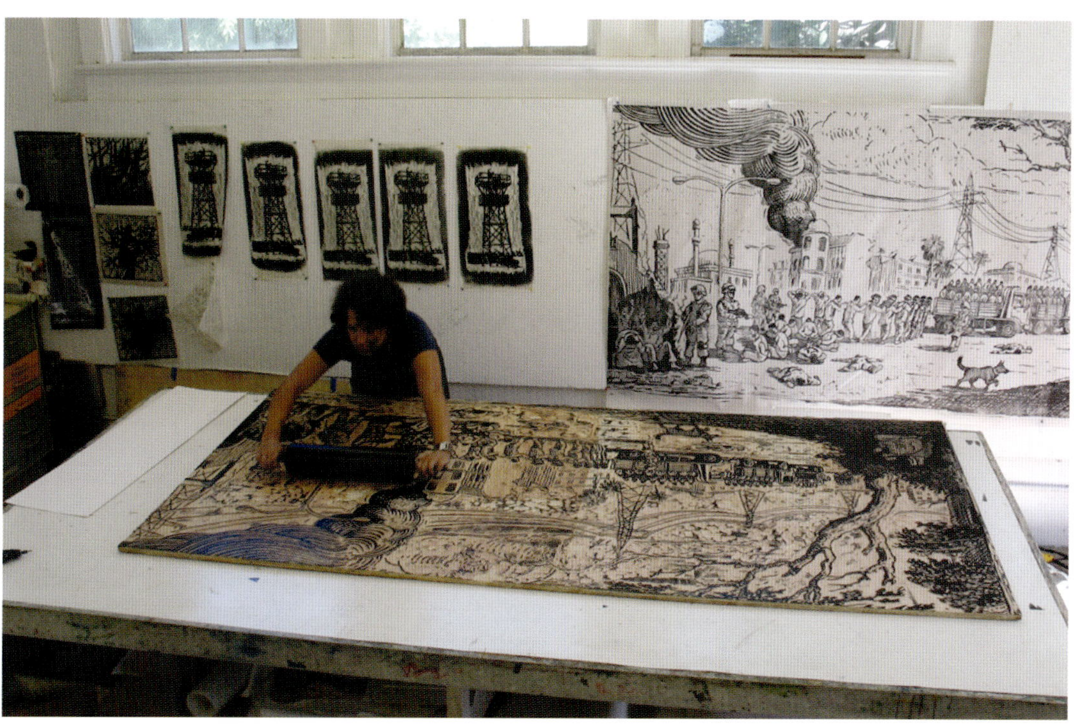

Nichol Markowitz

The Depravities of War

A series of large-scale woodcut prints produced at HuiPress, Hui Noʻeau Visual Arts Center, Makawao, Hawaiʻi, by

Sandow Birk and Elyse Pignolet
Paul Mullowney, *Master Printer*
Casey Neumann, *Head Printer*
Katherine Godwin, *Assistant*
Samuel Carr-Prindle and Nichol Markowitz, *Rhode Island School of Design interns*

This book is copublished by HuiPress Publications and Grand Central Press.

Designer: David Hamma
Production Assistant: Katherine Godwin
Publication/Exhibition Consultant: Andrea Harris-McGee
Editor: Sue Henger
Sandow Birk *The Depravities of War* Photography: Tony Novak-Clifford
Studio Photography: Paul Mullowney and Tony Novak-Clifford
Sandow Birk Paintings Photography: Jeff Ikemiya, JLI Photo Imaging; courtesy Catharine Clark Gallery.
Jacques Callot, *The Miseries of War* reproduced courtesy of UCLA Grunwald Centre for Graphic Arts, Hammer Museum, Los Angeles.
George Wesley Bellows, *The Cigarette*, and Honoré Daumier, *Rue Transnonian*, reproduced courtesy of San Diego Museum of Art.

Printer: Prolong Press Ltd, China
First Printing September 2007

Many thanks go out to Koplin Del Rio Gallery, Catharine Clark Gallery, PPOW Gallery, University Art Museum of CSULB, Shaw Center for the Arts, Second Street Gallery, Katzen Arts Center, American University Museum, CSU Fullerton and all the generous contributors to this amazing project.

HuiPress Publications
Hui No'eau Visual Arts Center
2841 Baldwin Avenue, Makawao, Maui, Hawai'i 96768
808-572-6560
www.huipress.com

Grand Central Press
csuf Grand Central Art Center
125 N. Broadway, Santa Ana, California 92701
714-567-7233 714-567-7234
www.grandcentralartcenter.com

International Standard Book Number:
0-9771696-9-3
978-09771696-9-6

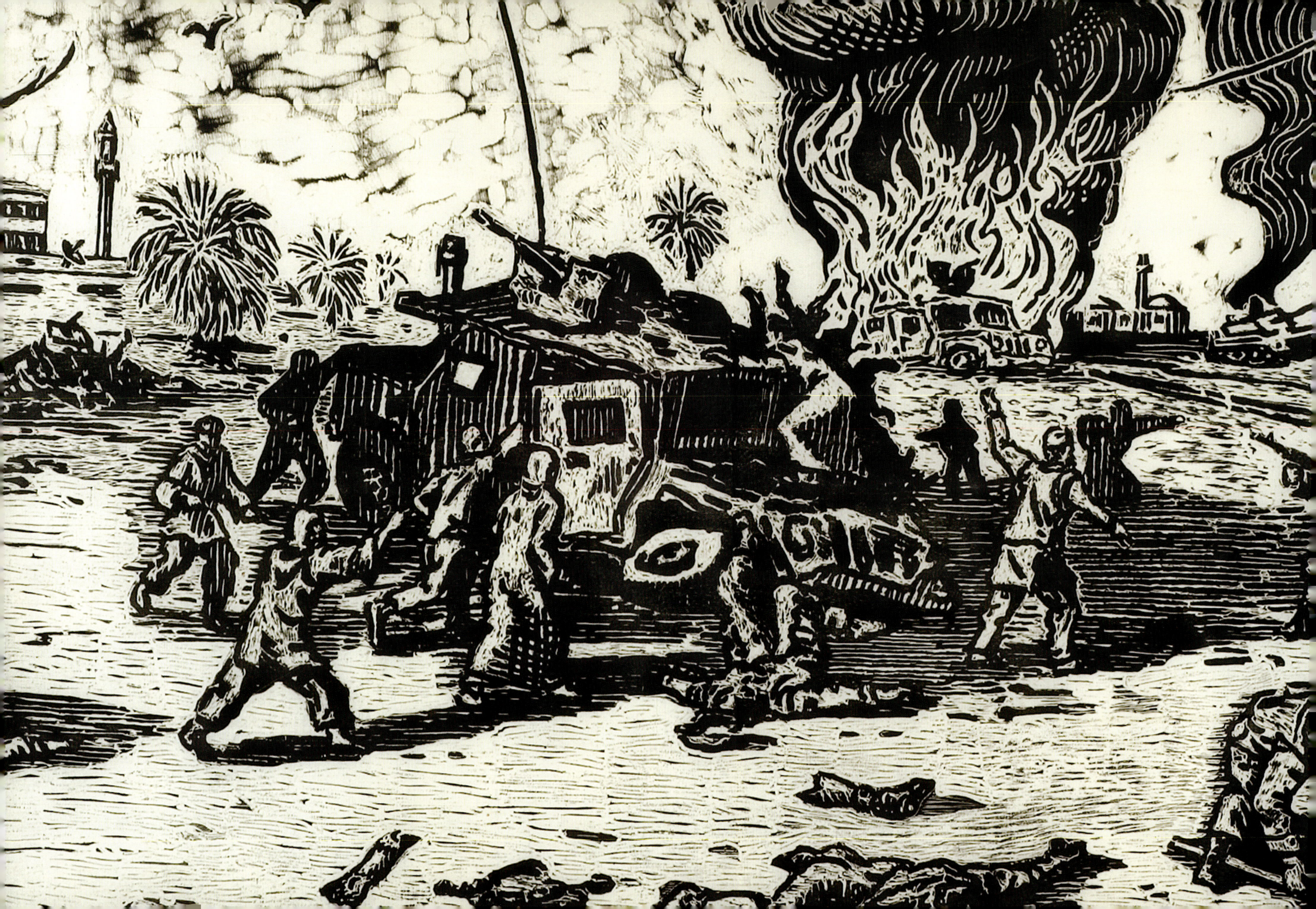